Quality

Tenets on Leadership

DR. RUSSELL LEO ROBERSON

Quality

Quality

Copyright © 2011

By

Dr. Russell Leo Roberson

Create Space

Nonfiction / Quality

First Edition (June, 2011)

First Printing (June, 2011)

Title ID: 3576610

ISBN-13: 978-1460982808

Quality

My Grandparents

William Harris, Sawyer

Lala Harris, Homemaker

Leo Roberson, Farmer

Lou Allie Roberson, Homemaker

Quality

Russell Roberson, Colonel USAF (retired)

Adelaide Roberson, Teacher

This book is dedicated, quite simply, to my parents and grandparents who taught me the value of focus, hard work and to never give up on a goal that I have set; traits that have served me well in my life and in my two battles with cancer.

Quality

Contents

Quality

Quality

Introduction

Before we get deep into this book and the concepts that follow, it might help to provide some background on myself – providing context on where the principles and concepts of this book are derived.

I have worked in the medical drug and device industry for close to 30 years. After graduating from Auburn University in 1981 with a Bachelor of Science degree in Agricultural Engineering, I began my career as a manufacturing engineer for a large food company; three years later (and with a Master of Science degree in Mechanical Engineering) I started my journey in the healthcare field as a quality engineer. Over the years, I have had responsibility for chemical and environmental laboratories, water and air systems, auditing, engineering, manufacturing and most recently as the Vice-President of quality for a medical drug and device organization. Along the way, I attained a Master of Business Administration degree and a Doctorate degree in Business Administration and Management. I am also a licensed Professional Engineer and hold, to date, six American Society of Quality certifications in the areas of

Quality

engineering, auditing and quality management. Since 1996, I have been an adjunct professor at several universities where I instruct in the areas of quality, statistics, strategy, change management, ethics and mathematics. I have found teaching helps me stay at the top of the knowledge pyramid in my field. I am also a frequent speaker at global conferences, where I have presented much of the material in this book (e.g. the material in chapter 12 of this book is from a presentation I gave at the American Society of Quality World Quality Conference in 2010; if you are interested a video clip is available regarding this the ASQ presentation; which can be found at the web link: http://www4.asq.org/qualityforlife/personal-stories/using-quality-to-battle-cancer---video.html). I have also published work in many formats from textbooks to journals.

I have applied the material in this book; this is a critical point – the material in this book has been tested and found to be practical and useful. As important, over the years I have had many of my students tell me that they have also applied the material in this book and they, also, have found the material useful and sound. So, what you are about to read is ready made for application! Professionally, I have had the privilege of working on products and services that provide value to patients and their caregivers; realizing that the same products and services could also be the source of irreversible harm. This is a responsibility that I have not taken lightly. This hit

home with me during my two battles with

cancer (non-Hodgkin's Lymphoma) in

1991 and 2006. I have used the same

products that I have helped design,

manufacture and distribute to help save

my own life. If you are interested, I have

published a book on my journey with

cancer (<u>Cancer: A Journey With Dignity and Honor</u>) that is available

on amazon.com. It is one thing to develop and apply quality tools, it

is quite another to have to use the same quality tools to help deliver

life-saving care for yourself; I think this unique opportunity has

shaped the way I think about quality and my profession.

Quality is my passion – it is more than my profession –

quality is my purpose – developing and implementing the concepts

of quality is how I give back to the society in which I live. It is really

that simple – I have spent my life in the quality field; I have worked

my way to significant levels of responsibility and have developed

processes that I think can be used in any industry and in the

personal lives of most anyone. I hope you will find this to be true – I

encourage you to look for applications in each chapter of this book –

Quality

I think you will find each chapter offers a seed that if planted and nurtured can, within time, improve the quality systems of your organization.

Thank you for taking the time to read this book. Now, let's get started on our journey into the field of quality!

The Eielson AFB Tigers – where I learned my first lessons related to teamwork.

Learning a bit of wisdom from my father on the Alaska – Canada highway (1968)

SECTION I

STRATEGY

The Wisdom Tradition Model

Over my career, I have had the opportunity to transform organizations; transformations that were both immediate and long-term. Both transformation types are equally as important and equally as difficult. Many years ago I developed the Wisdom to Tradition model to guide me in these transformation journeys; this is the model that I want to share with you in chapter 1 of this book.

It should come as no surprise that the culture of an organization is, by far, the overriding factor in the success or failure of any strategy – culture overrides everything about strategy – culture, quite simply, consumes strategy, chews it up and spits it out. The beauty of the Wisdom to Tradition model is that the impact of an organization's culture is taken into account as the organization seeks to transform itself. The Wisdom to Tradition model is perpetual, cycling through itself many times in the life of an organization; each time with a different spin and a different set of inputs and outputs – all dependent on the organizational culture, the competitive environment in which the organization operates, the talent mix of the organization and other organizational factors.

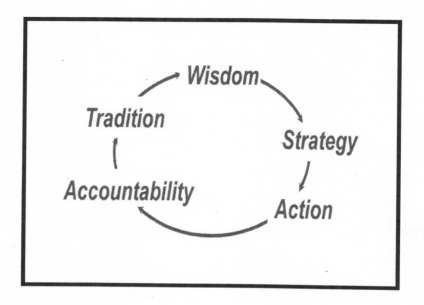

Let's start with a few simple questions and then deep dive into the Wisdom to Tradition model. We will examine the meaning of each term in the model and then answer the question why the Wisdom to Tradition model is perpetual.

Tradition: This is the starting point of the Wisdom to Tradition model. Every organization has traditions; traditions which embody the culture of the organization. Tradition has many indicators – from the way an organization designs, builds, distributes and services their products and services to how the organization treats their stakeholders. It is critical that the traditions of the organization be understood, at a deep level, before any attempt is made to deploy the Wisdom to Tradition Model.

Quality

→ tribal knowledge

Wisdom: Every individual and organization has some level of wisdom based upon historical knowledge and experience. Wisdom can either be purchased (by hiring from outside, using consultants, through external training and more) or it can be developed internal to the organization. It is critical that the organization attract and develop the proper wisdom at the proper internal to external ratio.

Strategy: A top level strategy (goals, objectives, long-term planning, etc.) should be developed using the collective wisdom of the organization. The better the wisdom of the organization, the better the strategy will be.

Action: Strategy drives action; which in the Wisdom to Tradition model is defined as the tactical plans developed to support the strategy. Tactical plans must be specific in nature; detailed actions with timelines and with individuals assigned as accountable.

Accountability: Actions require accountability – accountability is the achievement of the plan; on schedule, in a detailed and defensible manner. Accountability only works when achieving the plan is rewarded; and failure to achieve the plan is punished.

Tradition: Understanding the tradition of the organization, and then utilizing the steps of wisdom, strategy, action and accountability helps transform the traditions of the organization. At first the transformation may be small; yet any movement as a designed function of the Wisdom to Tradition model is good – eventually leading to an organization tradition structure that is sustainable – that provides a competitive advantage for the organization. The next step in the model, wisdom, is affected by the traditions of the firm – and the model repeats itself over and over again.

The Wisdom to Tradition model can be quite difficult to implement; taking years to fully complete enough cycles to effectively change the culture of the organization – and from there sustain the resultant culture. This process can be quite stressful as the organization begins to understand that the current wisdom and traditions of the organization may not be the wisdom and traditions needed in order for the organization to thrive and be competitive in the current or future environment. Now that there is a basic level understanding of the Wisdom to Tradition model, let's dig a bit deeper into each section of the model.

Quality

The element of tradition starts with the process of investigation; investigation into the current culture of the organization and the underlying causes. Research, followed by observation and concluded by experimentation provides a proper investigation process for the element of tradition. All of these steps take considerable time and thought.

Research is a lonely event; starting with a deep dive into understanding the purpose of the organization, followed by a stakeholder analysis of how the organization is viewed and then a determination of areas for  observation and experimentation. A starting place for understanding the purpose is linking the mission statement of the organization to its current goals and objectives; which includes the analysis of the metrics associated with the goals and objectives. Metrics are a critical indicator of the organization's actual purpose; as opposed to an organization's stated purpose that is found in their mission statement. I have found that it is helpful to start the analysis of purpose with a few questions; such as:

1. Are all of the organization's stated purposes found in the metrics of the organization?
2. How often are metrics taken and analyzed?
3. Which metrics get more attention by the different management levels of the organization?
4. What metrics turn into actions; what metrics just linger regardless of their output?
5. What is the action taken for a metric that is not achieved – does the organization act strongly to achieve the metric or does the organization accept the failure – acting as if the failure never happened.

Now, this is not the only list of questions – just an example of the type of questions that are helpful. The key here is find out how linked are the stated purpose of the organization and the way the organization actually behaves. This type of information leads to the successful analysis of internal and external stakeholders.

Stakeholder analysis, as part of the research tenet of tradition, can range from reviewing employee survey feedback to customer feedback, from reviewing legal and oversight body reports to the review of public information about the organization. What does all this information say about the organization? Is the organization respected; does the organization seek to fully satisfy its stakeholders or does the organization ride the fine line between right and wrong? What is the attitude of stakeholders – is there a sense of pride as a result of being associated with the organization? What is the level of self-esteem of the employees of the organization – are they positioned to add value to the organization, do they have the knowledge to add value to the organization, do they have the desire to add value to the organization? From here, the natural extension is to examine the operational systems of the organization – what are the dominant rules of the organization, what processes dominate the way the organization thinks and acts?

The determination of areas for observation and experimentation is an important decision. Areas for observation and experimentation should be focused where there are disconnects between the purpose of the organization and the metrics of the organization; where tension exist in the stakeholder relationships, where there are significant legal – oversight body concerns and on the dominant operational systems of the organization. So, if an organization's focus is design – then observation and experimentation related to the design systems of the organization would be proper. More than likely there will be many areas for observation and experimentation; the areas should be selected carefully with attention paid to those areas that have the most significant impact on the culture of the organization.

Observation is much more than just walking around and watching how the systems of the organizations operate; how the stakeholders of the organization act and interact. Observation  requires a laser focus – in a few key areas – rather than general observation across a wide range of areas. The output of research provides this focus; observation should not occur until the proper focus areas are identified. Observation only works after research has been properly conducted; move into the observation stage too quickly and the conclusions of the observation stage will not be useful; in fact the observations will more than likely be harmful. Just as important, it is critical that the observers of tradition be qualified – in the core areas of the organization – human resources, design, operations, service and the like. Observation is a team event.

Observation should not be done in private; observation

should be done in full public view. This can be done by attending meetings where metrics are discussed – at all levels of the organization. This can be done by attending meetings where the dominant systems of the organization are deployed. This can be done by absorbing how the organization reacts to and responds to legal – oversight body concerns. Observation is not about what is being done, but more about the how of what is being done happens. Is there total commitment to the actions of the organization, do stakeholders have the proper input and influence? What happens after a decision is made – does support for the decision continue after the decision was made? How deep into the organization are the decisions communicated – what are the methods of communication? The output of the observation stage will lead to hypotheses about the culture of the firm – a hypothesis that can be tested through experimentation.

Experimentation naturally follows research and observation. Experimentation must be designed to verify or reject a hypothesis; the results of experimentation must lead to a determination of the type of wisdom the organization must purchase or build in order make the improvements needed for the organization to prosper. For this to happen, the element of experimentation must adhere to a structured plan, where the information utilized is both accurate and without bias. Linking to the design system observation example earlier, a hypothesis might be generated that the process of in-depth data review for product or service design is not at the proper depth (i.e. H_1: There is not a proper in-depth review of data at product and service design reviews). This hypothesis would be based upon the research showing the design system as dominant and an observation showing that in-depth data reviews are an indicator of the organizational culture as related to the system of design. From this point, specific projects would be selected that have the potential for an in-depth data review. Next, there must be specific acts or actions that will be used to analyze the results – so, in order to determine if there were sufficient in-depth data reviews during design data collection there must be a criteria for judgment – e.g. the time allotted to data review, the number of findings associated with the data review, the attitude of participants during a data review, et al. The key is that the measures must be defined before experimentation begins and that the measures must be constant in all of the samples used during the experimentation. It is up to the organization to select the measures, but they must select measures for this process to work. Given the result of the experimentation, the alternate hypothesis will be confirmed or

Quality

rejected – it matters not which as experimentation seeks to understand – not to favor any one particular outcome.

Given the result of experimentation, it is now possible to define the traditions of the organization and some, but not all, of the underlying causes. It is the identification of underlying causes that will be critical in the decisions regarding purchasing and building wisdom. Using the design system example, if in four of five design reviews it was noted that data reviews were inadequate, if the time devoted to the data review was insufficient and if any challenges to the adequacy of the data review were confirmed (and by whom) then the hypothesis (H_1) that the process of in-depth data review (during design) is insufficient would be confirmed. This could be the result of many factors; such as inadequate technical knowledge of the participants, a conflict of time available for the data review with another priority or perhaps even that there are participants that inhibit the discussion of data at an in-depth level. The key is that once the H_1 hypothesis has been confirmed (or rejected) there must be an investigation to determine the reason for the decision.

All of this – research, observation and experimentation – leads to the determination of the culture of the organization – which will be the basis for the decisions to follow.

Quality

Wisdom

The element of wisdom is fed by the output of tradition; then decisions must be made regarding the acceptable pace of change within the organization along with the type of stakeholders and stakeholder relationships necessary to sustain the acceptable pace of change. This will lead to the decision on which systems of the organization require change in the short and long term and, from this point, whether to purchase talent from outside the organization or to build the talent from within the organization. So, the wisdom process entails:

1. take the inputs from the tradition element,
2. determine the pace of acceptable change,
3. determine the type of stakeholder and stakeholder relationships that will sustain the desired change, and
4. decide on which dominate systems to change and make the purchase / build decision regarding talent.

The input from the tradition element is just that – an input, a recommendation. It is important to understand that it takes wisdom to interpret the recommendations of the tradition element. In the first cycle of the Wisdom to Tradition model, this can be a very difficult task; but as the model cycles the interpretation of the tradition element becomes easier. The key is to look at the inputs from the element of tradition holistically; what does the information say about the culture of the organization; what is the patience for change in the organization, what has to change immediately and what can change over time?

The pace of acceptable change is a critical decision. Acceptable change takes many forms – from the change that must happen immediately (e.g. change required by legal entities and oversight bodies or change required to keep customers purchasing the products and services of the organization) to change that is acceptable over time (e.g. changes to a dominate system of the operation). Each change has a set of talents required to implement and sustain the change; so knowing what the changes must be is critical to the subsequent decisions regarding talent. The changes that need to happen in the organization must be seen as necessary and evident by the organization's stakeholders; the changes must be communicated in a clear and concise manner, over and over again to the stakeholders of the organization. At this point is it not important to define change other than by the terms immediate, short-term and long-term; during the strategy element of the Wisdom to Tradition model the time of each change will be further defined.

Determining the type of stakeholder and stakeholder relationships that will sustain the desired change requires an analysis of the type of individual(s) and organization(s) that will champion the change(s). This decision carries with it the indication of additions to and removals from the organization's staff and / or stakeholder lists. Continuing with the design system example, the type of individual that might be needed to improve the design process might be someone with strong technical knowledge, someone who understands how others in the industry operate design systems, someone who has experience with the change process necessary to change a dominate system of an organization and, most important, someone who believes that change is needed if the organization is to prosper. This analysis extends to stakeholders; e.g. the type of suppliers that provide goods and services to an organization must fit the proper characteristics of a supplier. After the complete stakeholder analysis has been completed, the next step is to examine how the mix of talent will interact. It is not enough to have the proper talent; the proper talent must be able to function together in such a manner to drive the changes required in the organization – using as a roadmap the strategy developed through the strategy stage of the Wisdom to Tradition model. Deviations from the strategic plans established cannot happen; if this were to occur then the organizational focus would be spread like a shotgun shell; the precision of the actions would be unacceptable. In this stage of the wisdom to tradition model, job requirements are set and established; requirements that will be used to help make the all-important purchase or build decision relative to talent.

Now that there have been decisions made on the pace of change and the type of stakeholder necessary to implement and sustain the change, it is now appropriate to decide on which dominate systems to change. This decision affects the amount and type of talent that must be purchased and built. The decision on which dominate systems to change fit into three distinct categories:

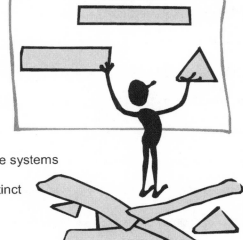

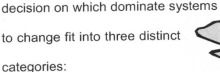

1. what has to be changed in order to comply with applicable laws and regulations,

2. what has to be changed in order to assure customer satisfaction with the organization's goods and services, and

3. what has to be changed in order to change the culture of the organization?

Change is not easy – most everyone is for change except when the change has an impact on them! Yet, change is needed – this book is an example – as we will discuss in chapter 6 there has been little change in the field of deep quality thought in the past sixty years! Change associated with laws and regulations is easy to implement – these are not negotiable and reasonable people get the need to be compliant. Change associated with customer satisfaction requires that the employees of the organization recognize the value of the correct customers to be greater than any agenda that they might personally have. Changes related to culture are the most difficult changes of all – this type of changes affect the core of the organization and often require deep sacrifices. All three categories are important; the Wisdom to Tradition model is about changing and sustaining an organization – for this to happen all three categories of change must be embraced.

The final element of the Wisdom stage is the decision regarding purchasing and building talent. Implied in this element is the decision to remove talent from the organization; and rest assured there will be a need to remove some amount of talent from the organization – either as a function of talent that does not meet the requirements of the jobs or as a function of talent that has outgrown their current roles in the organization. Purchased talent can be external or internal to the organization; such a talent hired into the organization from other organizations or talent utilized on assignment from other areas within the organization. There will need to be some level of purchased talent in every cycle of the Wisdom to Tradition model. Built talent is solely internal to the organization; where there is reasonable hope that with the proper focus, training and mentorship that an employee will attain the required level of job expertise. It is critical to invest in building talent in every cycle of the Wisdom to Tradition model; building talent builds employee confidence and self-esteem – which is needed if the organization is to prosper – given that there is only so much talent that can be purchased. The proper purchase to build talent ratio varies with each cycle of the Wisdom to Tradition model – in the early cycles the purchase to build ratio will be higher than in later cycles – as the organization gets better and better at hiring, educating, training and mentoring its employees. The types of talent that must leave the organization, in the early cycles, are:

1. those that do not support the changes necessary,)
   .

2. ones that look to undermine the direction of the organization, or (
   .

3. talent that is not qualified to perform the roles needed in the organization. ｜
   .

In the early cycles of the Wisdom to Tradition model, it is better to err on the side of removing too many than too few; there cannot be a battle for leadership. In the later cycles of the Wisdom to Tradition model, an appropriate balance naturally happens – with managed exits reaching the level of industry average.

It is the accumulation of the proper wisdom that sets the stage for the next part of the Wisdom to Tradition model – that being Strategy.

this can take years

Quality

Strategy

Strategy happens as a result of the wisdom of the organization. Strategy is not tactical; tactical happens in the next stage of the Wisdom to Tradition model (i.e. Action). The strategic stage focuses on the establishment of goals and objectives for the organization; relative to the immediate, short-term and long-term. For organizations in the early cycles of the Wisdom to Tradition mode, the establishment of goals and objectives can be a difficult endeavor – in the later cycles the establishment of goals and objectives gets easier as the organization becomes more and more receptive to the concept.

Establishing goals and objectives is difficult for many reasons – the personalities involved in the goals and objectives process can be diverse – as a result of the decisions made in the wisdom stage of the Wisdom to Tradition model. Yet, this process should be difficult – as difficult processes offer great opportunity for learning and it is this learning that will help future cycles of the Wisdom to Tradition model go smoother. Strong leadership is critical in order to assure proper goals and objectives are established – leadership that has focus on the changes required but that also allows constructive and dynamic debate on the process

Quality

of change. The goals and objectives should be centered on a set of core values; e.g. customer satisfaction, operational excellence, stakeholder sustainment, adherence to applicable laws and the like. This will make the task of setting specific goals and objectives easier. An important and necessary part of the goals and objective process is the establishment of specific metrics – with a success and effectiveness requirement for each and every metric. As important the metrics must support the changes needed in the organization; they must be the catalyst that drives performance and actions. Using the design system example, a goal and objective might be that product released does not result in a future defect that would require an unanticipated update – the metric in the first cycle of the Wisdom to Tradition model might be a success rate of 80% of the design programs achieve this goal and objective; in future cycles the success rate might reach 100% for this goal and objective.

Strategic planning is best done off site; in a location that offers solitude for the participants – where participants can focus on the business of strategic planning without the interruptions of their daily work. It is important that during these strategy sessions the focus is not limited to the immediate, short-term or long-term; this can be sorted out later. I define immediate goals as less than one year, short-term goals as one to three years and long-term goals as three to five year in length. Each type of goal should be an outcome of the strategy session; it is not enough to just think about strategy in the immediate term. Having short-term and long-term goals also helps an organization understand the advancement that has happened as the Wisdom to Tradition cycle repeats itself. This approach helps organizations plan actions that meet all three strategic terms (immediate, short-term and long-term). An example of where this would be in the development of internal talent. An immediate goal might be a talent assessment and enough training and mentorship to meet the minimum performance requirements, a short-term goal might be the structured education of employees with well-designed projects and interactions to foster performance at the exceptional level and the long-term goal might be talent of the organization is of such depth and diversity that the talent, itself, is a strong tool used by the organization when they recruit talent. Another example, this time for a long-term goal might be the creation of a technically excellent engineering department, with highly qualified engineers, who have a deep understanding of the goods and services of the organization, who understand how products and services are used and misused. All goals time frames need metrics; the immediate and short-term goals need metrics that are specific whereas the long-term goals do not need a specific metric. With long-term goals, the goal itself sends the clear message that dramatic change must happen; some will get this message and improve; others will get this message and leave – in either case the organization, the stakeholder(s) and the customer(s) prosper.

Of critical importance with respect to the development of a strategy is the understanding that the strategy of the organization must match what the culture of the organization will support; this requires tempering the strategy and subsequent actions – prudent patience is critical in the implementation of the Wisdom to Tradition model. This means that the pace of change in the dominant systems of the organization may take several cycles of the Wisdom to Tradition model. From my experience, there are six distinct stages of culture, those being:

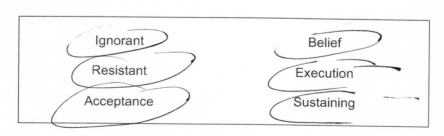

Quality

It is possible to move through multiple culture stages in one cycle of the Wisdom to Tradition model; or to need multiple cycles of the Wisdom to Tradition model to move through one type of culture. It is also possible to move backwards in the culture stages. Details of my defined culture type are as follows:

Ignorant

> Organization lacks self-awareness; does not see impending doom; overestimates knowledge; ego overrules proper judgment

> Organization does not see the need for change

> Improper stakeholders believe they are indispensible and invincible

Quality

Resistant

> ➢ Organization understands current strategy will not work; remains in denial believing external environments are the reason to blame organizational difficulties.
>
> ➢ Organization invents obstacles to change; purposely slows down improvements
>
> ➢ Stakeholders find organization difficult to work with

Acceptance

> ➢ Organization understands that without change the organization will not survive
>
> ➢ Organization implements change without understanding why the changes are necessary; change is based on blind faith in the leadership of the organization
>
> ➢ The pace of change is noticeable to the proper stakeholders

Quality

Belief

> Organization tips - understands the strategic direction is proper; understands the logic of the strategy

> The need for change in understood and embraced; those remaining individuals who oppose change leave the organization.

> The proper stakeholders believe they have a critical part to play in the success of the organizational strategy; stakeholder motivation and commitment increases; stakeholders have a passion for the success of the organization

Execution

> Improvements happen at a quick and prudent pace; actions identified are met on time, within budget

> Talent links strongly to the strategy and actions of the organization

> The proper stakeholders notice the changes and agree the changes are proper

Quality

Sustaining

> ➤ Tradition sets in; ignorance no longer continues to exist.
>
> ➤ Strategic planning, actions and accountability are the expectations of the proper stakeholders
>
> ➤ Knowledge and logic are used for prudent decision making based on agreed upon metrics

Think of it based on power

Another way to think about my dimensions of culture is through a power grid. In the ignorant and resistant stages, power is authoritative with little or no constructive conflict – groupthink at its worst. In the acceptance stage, power is legitimate – resting on the reporting relationships established by the organization. In the belief stage, power is both legitimate and referent as stakeholders gain respect for the leadership of the organization. In the execution and sustaining stages, power is shared by those in the organization – a matrix reporting environment exists – with accountability directly to the goals and objectives of the organization. In the execution and sustaining stages both success and failure are easily visible.

Quality

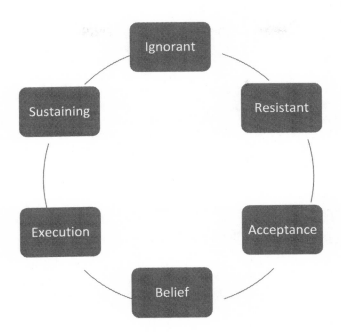

The output of the strategy stage must link directly to the current culture of the organization and the expected culture that the leadership of the organization believes will be achieved at the end of the Wisdom to Tradition cycle. In many cases, the first cycle of the Wisdom to Tradition model seeks to transform the culture form ignorant to acceptance, then belief to execution in the second cycle and achieve sustaining culture in the third cycle. The output of the strategy stage leads to the specific actions needed to accomplish the stated goals and objectives; actions that are tactical in nature.

Quality

Action

The Action stage of the Wisdom to Tradition model establishes the tactical plans to support the strategy. The tactical plans of the Action stage must be specific in nature; with timelines and with individuals assigned as accountable. So, what does a specific plan look like – how much detail and depth is required? The simple answer is the more detail and depth the better; the better answer is enough detail and depth to assure there are clear milestones that push the plan to completion at the assigned time and achieve the culture transformation desired by the strategic plan.

Tactical planning goes across a breadth of areas – from the problem statement to how effectiveness will be measured, from how updates will be communicated and messaged to the knowledge of precedent conditions for each stage of the action plan. There can be many ways to achieve a strategic goal – driving the goal to a tactical action plan requires development of multiple options to address the purpose of the goal. Using this approach, selections can be made to assure the tactical plan will accomplish the purpose of the strategic goal. For example, if a strategic goal was to improve the quality of product changes, there could be many possible action plan options – the redesign of the total design control process, the redesign of the design control process associated with change control, the education of the workforce that is associated with product changes, et al. The choice of an action plan or action plans is a critical choice; the best strategy will not survive an inappropriate action plans.

Taking the time to define the action plan is well worth the effort – starting with defining exactly what problem the action plan is intending to solve. This analysis should result in a specific result; e.g. the reduction of a specific defect or defects in a specific product line. The action plan should, at a minimum, include the elements of:

1. Problem definition

2. Communication; information sharing; progress, et al

3. An analysis of the talent required to complete the action plan

4. Specific deliverables; with appropriate contingency planning

5. A method of asking for help and guidance on a routine basis

6. A method for measuring the success or failure of each stage

7. A method to determine if the outcome is sustainable and effective

In a later chapter in this book entitled SWEATT (strengths, weaknesses, excellence, actions, threats and teamwork) the process of defining actions and measures associated with the strategic plan is discussed; along with a concept known as movement points – the point at which an element moves to another dimension of the SWEATT model. The specific actions, timelines and accountability determination feed the next stage of the Wisdom to Tradition model – accountability.

Quality

Accountability

Accountability is the achievement of the action plan; on schedule, in a detailed and defensible manner. Accountability only works when achieving the plan is rewarded and failure to achieve the plan is punished. Accountability requires significant and focused oversight at multiple levels within the organization at critical stages of the action plan. Relative to accountability, there is an inherent expectation that contingency planning is done to assure the commitments of the action plan are met as scheduled. This is not to imply perfection is the only acceptable result; it is acceptable to modify an action plan under the proper oversight. Yet, there is a limit to modifications. There must be little if no tolerance for the failure to achieve the commitments of the action plan when contingencies and reasonable modifications are taken into account. This is a critical and paradigm shifting event – there must be accountability for the action plans – timely, visible and meaningful. It is the accountability section of the Wisdom to Tradition model that delivers the culture change desired and the resultant traditions of the organization. Accountability can range from the positive (e.g.

positive comments, communications, non-financial and financial rewards, celebration, etc.) to the constructive (e.g. comments expressing dissatisfaction, a requirement for more frequent and deeper action plan reviews with leadership, the transfer or removal of individual(s) from their roles within the organization, the lack of celebrations, etc.). Holding stakeholders accountable is not an easy task; but this is a necessary step – leadership must understand that the failure to hold the right individuals accountable is, in fact, doing an extreme disservice to those individuals that are being fully accountable to their own action plan. Leaders succeed and fail as a direct result of their:

1. ability to think strategically,

2. build talent, and

3. specify metrics for which they hold the organization accountable

All three elements must happen for a leader to succeed; just one failure of the elements above and the leader will fail. If the leader fails – the organization fails – enough said!

Quality

Defensible accountability is a measure of how others who are independent of those being held directly accountable will view the results of the action plan. This includes the written and oral presentation of the action plan results. Properly defensible written action plans should be presented in the format of a well written report; with executive summaries and detail of the action plan activities with conclusions. It is a written action plan that helps others who are independent of the action plan to determine if the actions taken were proper and complete; along with providing the detail needed to assure organizational learning. Properly defensible oral action plans requires the training of the action plan teams and individuals in the skill set of communications at the appropriate level of depth relative to the receiving audience.

Accountability – as the culture of the organization matures from ignorant to sustainable – will transcend from the responsibility of leadership to those that that are accountable to the action plan – all in a journey to change the traditions of the organization.

Tradition

With tradition, the Wisdom to Tradition cycle repeats itself – restarting the process of investigation, research and experimentation. The restart of the Wisdom to Tradition model is not something that happens naturally – the process of organizational self-examination must be planned and implemented in each cycle of the model as meticulously as the cycles before. With each Wisdom to Tradition cycle the outputs of each stage should be stronger and more closely linked to the culture the organization's leadership has envisioned.

Conclusion

The Wisdom to Tradition model is a fitting first chapter for this book; the chapters that follow provide further insight into areas of the Wisdom to Tradition model – e.g. the SWEATT model helps link strategy and action plans, the 4-D model (Discovery, Discuss, Decide and Document) links the concepts of tradition and strategy, the identification of the proper and improper stakeholders links to the strategy of the organization, the responsibility of the organization to define quality links to the strategy and action plans, and the ten characteristics of an effective leader links to the concepts of responsibility – which embodies the Wisdom to Tradition model holistically.

The
SWEATT
Model

When I demonstrate the SWEATT (Strengths, Weaknesses, Excellence, Actions, Threats and Team) model I often get the feedback that the SWEATT model takes the tool of SWOT (Strengths, Weaknesses, Opportunities and Threats) and actually makes SWOT useful. I find the SWOT model inadequate; due to the lack of detail in a SWOT model and the tendency to use the SWOT model as a brainstorming tool rather than a strategic tool. SWEATT was developed out of necessity; out of the desire to link the concepts of SWOT with realistic strategic planning – realism that becomes evident when metrics are linked to each element of the SWEATT model.

The SWEATT model utilizes the best practices of strategy and measurement to help drive a culture change in the organization. This SWEATT model has significant differences from the SWOT model – e.g. the SWEATT model focuses on defining a movement point for each identified area and action. SWEATT is an appropriate name for this model as the use of this model takes tremendous honesty, courage and compassion; it is not easy to self-access an organization nor is it easy for those who are embedded in an organization's culture to listen to or be part of a SWEATT analysis – for systems that they have been part of, or maybe even have helped develop and nurture, over a period of years – the SWEATT model will certainly makes those who use the model perspire (or sweat).

The SWEATT model utilizes the following format (using customer satisfaction as an example):

Focus Area	Measure	Current Value	Movement Point
Customer Satisfaction	Customer Satisfaction Survey Results	97%	93%

Let's start with a description of the elements of the SWEATT model and then move on to how the model can be utilized.

Strengths: The strength section of the SWEATT model is where the past successes of the organization are listed. The first pass at the strengths section may include items that are better listed as a weakness. Strengths can be either legitimate or ego based, the later inhibiting the quality improvement process of the organization. The second and subsequent passes at the strength section should include more items that are legitimate and fewer items that are ego based.

Quality

Weaknesses: The weakness section of the SWEATT model is where the soul searching of the organization takes place. In order for this section to be of value, there must be no organizational system or process that is off limits; this includes the competence of the current senior leadership team, the current goals of the organization and the current human and technical resource talent of the organization. In the first pass of the SWEATT model weaknesses section, the weaknesses listed may be superficial; but as the SWEATT model matures the elements of the weakness should become more honest, and thus, beneficial.

Excellence: The excellence section of the SWEATT model encompasses the objectives that, if achieved, will offer a significant improvement to the organization's products, services and processes. The excellence section differs from the opportunity section of the classic SWOT model in that the excellence section of the SWEATT model encompasses significant improvements that are plausible and possible, whereas the opportunity section of the SWOT model encompasses that may be nether plausible or possible. The elements of excellence are the game changer for the organization in a positive way. If excellence events were to occur they would drive a significant competitive advantage for the organization.

Actions: The action section of the SWEATT model encompasses the actions necessary to maintain the strengths of the organization, decrease the weaknesses of the organization, achieve the excellence objectives of the organization and avoid the threats under which the organization operates. The actions identified in this section must be achievable. There should also be a mix of immediate (less than one year), short-term (one to three years) and long-term (three to five years).

Threats (T): The threat section of the SWEATT model encompasses the events that, if they happen, could prevent the organization for improving their products, services and processes. The threats must be based in reality; there must be a reasonable chance the threats could actually occur if actions are not taken to prevent them from happening. The elements of the threat section are also game changers for the organization – in a negative manner. If threat events were to occur they would result in a competitive disadvantage for the organization.

Team: The team member section provides the next level of management with an indication of biases under which the SWEATT model was developed. The SWEATT model will only be as good as the team that works the model; the wrong SWEATT team can do tremendous damage to the SWEATT model and, from there, tremendous damage to the quality strategy of the organization.

Now, to address the subsections of each SWEATT category:

Focus Area: The focus area is the specific area that has been identified as part of the S, W, E or T section of the SWEATT model. For example, an organization may focus on customer satisfaction as a strength or engineering talent in the weakness areas.

Measure: The measure is the attribute or variable of interest by which the focus area will be judged. For example, a customer satisfaction survey might be a measurement for customer satisfaction or the level of product experience might be a measurement of engineering talent.

Current Value: This is the current value of the measurement. For example, if the customer satisfaction survey rating was currently 97%, the current value would be 97%.

Movement Point: The movement point is where the measurement transfers from strength to a weakness, from a weakness to strength, from an opportunity to excellence or from a threat to reality. For example, if customer satisfaction were to fall to 93% and the organization felt that at this level customer satisfaction becomes a weakness, then the movement point is 93%.

Quality

The SWEATT model should start at a high level and move downward until the SWEATT model become actionable at the distinct levels (e.g. senior management, middle management and direct line management) of the organization and at distinct operations (e.g. manufacturing, service and marketing) within the organization. Each distinct operation of the organization should be able to use the cascading SWEATT model to develop a supporting quality strategy for their operation. I have found that with an organization that is need of a significant change it is best to develop a SWEATT model every four months for the first year (this establishes the process of the SWEATT model), then every six months for the next two years and then once year thereafter.

Well, enough on the theory of the SWEATT model; let's delve into an example of the SWEATT model and examine how the SWEATT model should be developed, nurtured and utilized to drive a competitive advantage for an organization. In the following pages, I have provided an example of each SWEATT element using as a basis an organization that manufactures a product.

Quality

Strengths

Focus	Measure	CV	MP
Product Development	# of New Products Introduced per Year	7	4
Quality	# of Product Recalls per Year	1	4
Talent	# of Recognized Thought Leaders - engineering / quality	9	8

Notes:

- New Products: Products which are listed in the strategic plan

- Recalls: As defined by the local country regulation; the same problem in multiple countries counts as one (1) recall

- Thought Leader: An individual who is able to influence the movement of the industry through their presence, writing, speeches, et al.

Quality

Weakness

Focus	Measure	CV	MP
Quality	Time Required to Investigate a Complaint To Root Cause (in days)	180	90
Global Markets	% of Markets where we have < 25% Market Share	80	25
Risk	# of internal Assessment Findings That Indicate a Major System Breakdown	12	2

Notes:

- Intend to Play: Any country where we have at a long-term strategic plan to own more than 25% of the market

Quality

Excellence

Focus	Measure	CV	MP
Predictive Modeling	# of Defects Predicted and Found Prior to Product Release	3	150
Influence	# of Committee Memberships in Which We Hold Significant Roles	5	15
Innovation	# of First to Market Innovations That Have Direct Impact on Ease of Customer Workflow	0	10

Notes:

- Significant Committee: A committee which is critical to ongoing and pending regulations that affect our industry (total available committees = 25)

- Customer Workflow: The manner in which the customer uses our products (e.g. keystrokes order of work, etc.)

Quality

Threats

Focus	Measure	CV	MP
Market Entry By Garage Based Software Firms	# of Firms Entering The Market That Are < 100M in Sales and Who Achieve At Least Two (2) Significant Sales	3	5
A Run on Talent	% of Critical Talent Enticed To Leave The Organization and Work For a Competitor	3	7
Failure to Regulate	The Lack of Regulation to Build a Barrier to Market Entry and By Doing So Endanger Public Safety	0	0

Notes:

- Critical Talent: Talent that is identified as critical to innovation and compliance

- "0" Value: The value of "0" relative to regulation indicates that no regulation exists

Quality

Actions

Focus	Measure	CV	MP
Assure Competitive Benefits	Restructure Bonus System as a % of Annual Pay	0	20
Global Market Penetration	Put On-The-Ground Talent in Markets Where Current Market Share < 25%; measure in # of employees	400	3800
Predictive Modeling	Test Run Four (4) Predictive Models on Multiple Product Lines; Measure Defects Detected and Severity of Defects	0	4

Notes:

- Bonus Systems: Bonuses to be paid base upon communicated and aggressive goals and objectives.

Quality

Team

Focus	Measure	CV	CV - 1
Leader	Years of Experience in the Industry	25	18
Mix of Expertise and Experience	Seasoned Representation from the areas of engineering, quality, regulatory, marketing, human resources, financial and operations	All Areas Present	Missing Operations
Metric	Expertise Available to Team Relative to Metric Determination and Analysis	Yes, Statistical Expert Utilized	No Statistical Expert Available

Notes:

- Team Members: This note would include the names of team members and their respective experience in the industry and with the organization.

Quality

There is a process to follow when implementing the SWEATT model; that being:

1. The selection of a SWEATT team

2. The training of the SWEATT team

3. Establishment of the SWEATT ground rules

4. Brainstorm first, then triage

5. Putting metrics around the critical mass

6. Sorting to the critical few

7. Use of notes to clarify

8. Linking the SWEATT model to immediate, short-term and long-term strategy

9. Communication of the SWEATT model

10. Repeating the SWEATT process

Quality

The **first step** in the SWEATT process is the selection of the SWEATT team. The SWEATT team should consist of a seasoned leader who has a significant vested interest in the outcome of the SWEATT process and a representative mix of expertise and experience. SWEATT team members must have constructive debate; without this the SWEATT team will fail. SWEATT team members must be strategic thinkers; individuals who think first of the investor and second of their own domain. Relative to the current value and current value minus one sections of the TEAM section of SWEATT, this is intended to provide information year over year on the competence of the SWEATT team. It is critical that the notes section of the TEAM section include the names of significantly contributing team members along with an attachment to the SWEATT model that provides more in-depth biographies of each team member. In future versions of the SWEATT model, understanding the differences in team structure and dynamics will help the current SWEATT team understand the logic and meaning behind previous SWEATT models.

Quality

The **second step** in the SWEATT process is the training of the SWEATT team. This is a critical step in the SWEATT process and should be repeated each period the SWEATT model is deployed. SWEATT model training should include the following:

➤ Element #1: The SWEATT Process

1. Understand the SWEATT model and the link to SWOT

2. Understand the terminology of the SWEATT model

3. Understand the importance of establishing proper metrics associated with each focus area

4. Understand the meaning of the movement point and the importance linking action to the movement point

5. Understand the importance of detailed notes as related to the SWEATT model

---

➤ Element #2: The SWEATT Strategy

1. Understand the importance of constructive debate and encouraging such

2. Understand the confidentiality of the SWEATT process

3. Link SWEATT to immediate, short-term and long-term strategy of the organization

4. Link SWEATT to the Wisdom to Tradition model

Quality

> ➤ **Element #3: Living With The SWEATT Model**
>
> 1. Communication and the SWEATT model
>
> 2. Using the SWEATT model to drive organizational improvement

This may seem like a lot of training – one hour should be the minimum time spent on the SWEATT process training; more than three hours would be too much. It is important to have the training each time the SWEATT model is used in order to assure the elements of SWEATT are properly understood and to ground any new team members in the SWEATT process.

Quality

The **third step** in the SWEATT process is the establishment of the SWEATT ground rules. The ground rules for the SWEATT model are quite simple:

1. The adage that there are not any stupid questions is completely wrong — there are plenty of stupid questions — none of which should be part of a SWEATT discussion (stupid questions are those that take the SWEATT team off track and for which the answer to the question is obvious and which add zero value to the discussion). This is why the SWEATT team was selected with the appropriate expertise and experience. SWEATT team members are expected to come to the SWEATT meeting well prepared with thoughtful suggestions for focus areas, metrics and movement points; SWEATT meetings should not be the first time a team member is thinking about the SWEATT process.

2. Debate should be respectful but challenging. The SWEATT model depends on challenging the assumptions of the past and the ideas of others. If there is not a constructive challenge to the idea of a fellow SWEATT team member, the SWEATT team should then name one team member to take an opposite view

and argue that point to assure the idea has been properly vetted.

3. SWEATT discussions must be confidential; as ideas and concepts of all types will be forthcoming – e.g. from the investment in Research and Development to the reduction of the workforce. In SWEATT language, this is known as walking around the problem – looking at the situation from many angles – even if the angle of view makes the SWEATT team momentarily uncomfortable.

4. SWEATT is a multiple day event; team members, depending on the level of the SWEATT model (e.g. from the highest strategic level to the departmental level) must be willing to devote between two – five days to the SWEATT model development.

Quality

The **fourth step** in the SWEATT process is to brainstorm, then triage. When the SWEATT team begins the process of idea generation there should be an assumption that the idea is worth listing. There is one caveat; the proposal of any idea must also include ideas for metrics. There should be no debate what-so-ever during the time when ideas and ideas for metrics are being proposed. This will most likely result in some areas being listed in multiple categories – e.g. in the example provided in this chapter the concept of Quality is listed as a strength and as a weakness. The separation point in the example is the metric. It is critical to allow ideas to flow during this time; as ideas build off each other. It is better to have too many ideas than too few to choose from as the SWEATT process moves to the triage stage.

Quality

The **fifth step** in the SWEATT process is putting metrics around the critical mass; this involves triaging out the ideas that, after review, do not warrant inclusion in the SWEATT model. The remaining ideas deserve a fair discussion – this means reflection on the proposed metric for each idea and, if necessary, modifying the metric to provide clarity with respect to the focus area. An important part of this discussion should be the metric itself, considering such items as:

1. the difficulty of obtaining the metric,

2. the difficulty of analysis with respect to the metric,

3. understanding how the metric can be linked to the goals and objectives of stakeholders,

4. understanding if the metric will inspire stakeholders to perform at higher than expected levels, and

5. understanding the value of the metric with respect to driving organizational improvements that will be noticed by the organization's customers and the organization's investors.

This step of the SWEATT process is the most time consuming; rush though this step of the SWEATT process and the team will find the resulting SWEATT is no more than a SWOT model.

Quality

The **sixth step** in the SWEATT process is sorting to the critical few. During this step, discussion will, and should continue, with respect to metrics. From my experience, in each SWEATT category there should be between five – seven items at the start of the SWEATT model period (items may move out of a particular category and into another category – however the total number of items in each category of the SWEATT model should remain, basically, the same); anything after the seventh choice should be pushed down to a lower level SWEATT model (e.g. from a divisional to a departmental SWEATT). The only exception to this is the ACTION category; which may require identified actions for each item (i.e. if there are five items in each SWEATT category, then a total of twenty actions might be required). It is also at this time that the current value of each SWEATT item must be identified along with the respective movement point. The success of step five of the SWEATT process drives the activities and outcome of step six of the SWEATT process. Without proper SWEATT items and associated metrics, it will be impossible to develop movement points that will actually drive actions that will improve the value of the organization. The SWEATT team must be certain that if, at any time, the movement point is breeched there is agreement on the movement of the item to another category of the SWEATT model and there are predetermined actions that will occur. This is a character defining moment for the SWEATT team; if they set movement points and then do not react properly at the time of the metric breech then the SWEATT model will lose its credibility – and with lost credibility the SWEATT model will become the SWOT model. I will use the SWEATT chart in this chapter as an illustration of these points:

1. Product development was listed as strength with a current value of seven and a movement point of four. This means that if the number of new products developed at end of year is equal to four then the product development item must be moved to the weakness category of the SWEATT model. Actions should be taken well before the movement points is breeched to prevent the item linked to product development from becoming a weakness; perhaps when the leadership of the organization realizes the potential of a movement point breech they might put more oversight and investment into specific products.

2. Quality was listed as a strength relative to recalls, with a current value of one and a movement point of four. This means that there is room for additional recalls beyond the current performance of the organization before quality becomes a

weakness. Again, if the breech point is foreseen, the organization must have a pre-set plan in place to prevent recalls reaching the n = 3 level.

3. Quality was also listed as a weakness relative to the time to resolve complaints to root cause, with a current value of 180 days and a movement point of 90 days. This means that for the organization to claim this item as a strength, the time taken to resolve complaints to root cause must reach the movement point; at 91 days the time to resolve complaints to root cause would still be considered a weakness. This is where the SWEATT model would link to immediate, short-term and long-term goals; it might not be possible to attain the movement point in one year, e.g. regardless, there should be specific action plans linked to the breaching of the movement point. Something should not be listed as a weakness that the organization is not committed to improve.

4. Influence was listed in the excellence section of the SWEATT model; this means if the movement point can be breached this item becomes an area of competitive advantage for the firm – in an area the firm is not currently seen as strong. The achievement of excellent movement points should be noticeable by the stakeholders of the organization and result in an

Quality

increased value of the organization. Again, the organization should have action plans directed a breeching the movement point; which may require multiple cycles of the SWEATT model to achieve.

5. A run on talent was listed in the threat section of the SWEATT model; this means if the movement points is breeched the threat has become significant and will have a direct impact on the organization – perhaps requiring a shift in the organizational strategy to compensate. In the example, if critical talent leaves the organization at a level greater than 7% this would result in a threat to the organization to maintain their items of strength or their ability to achieve excellence, e.g. There must be plans in place to prevent threats from becoming reality or, if there is no way to prevent this, plans should be in place to mitigate the impact of the threat (e.g. a retail store may not be able to prevent another store from locating in the same vicinity, but it could have plan in place to offset the threat through diversity of merchandise, etc.).

6. The restructuring of a bonus system was listed in the action segment of the SWEATT model with a current value of zero and a movement point of twenty. This means that the restructuring of the bonus system was linked to an item(s) in one of the other

SWEATT categories and that for the action plan to be successful the bonus plan must reach the 20% level.

These examples illustrate the linkage between the category, the item, the metric, the current value and the movement point – and the importance of the proper selection of each. Most organizations know how to run the plays they are given; the success or failure is often not in the execution stage but instead in the how success is defined. Mess this up and the SWEATT model actually detracts from the organization's ability to improve their value.

Quality

The **seventh step** of the SWEATT process is using the notes to clarify the items, metrics, current value and movement points. For example, in the notes section for threats the meaning of a "0" value for the time "failure to regulate" is defined. The notes section should be used to help clarify the meaning of the item, the metric and the values associated with the current value and movement points; and to provide context for future SWEATT models.

Quality

The **eighth step** of the SWEATT process is linking the SWEATT model to immediate, short-term and long-term strategy. As mentioned earlier, not all movement points will be breeched during one SWEATT cycle and, in fact, some movement points will, hopefully, never be breeched (e.g. movement points associated with strength). There may be subsets of action plans associated with the SWEATT model that links to the immediate, short-term and long-term strategy of the organization. If these time periods are not accounted for, then the SWEATT model would appear to overly optimistic – to the point that the credibility of the SWEATT model would be at risk.

Quality

The **ninth step** of the SWEATT process is the communication of the SWEATT model to at the appropriate level and content to the appropriate audience. Not all elements of the SWEATT model are appropriate for all audiences; e.g. the action plan relative to bonuses would not be appropriate to communicate broadly – as this action may change over the SWEATT period and, as such, could be seen as a demotivating rather than a motivator (e.g. if the bonus movement point were changed, due to improved information, from 20% to 15%). For those items of the SWEATT model that are appropriate to communicate, the SWEATT model should be posted and distributed. The SWEATT model is a window in the soul of the leadership of the organization and offers the stakeholders of the organization a view into how the organization believes it can achieve its mission. For example, if an organization's mission is to produce the best products at the best price and achieve exceptional customer satisfaction, the SWEATT model provides the insight into how the organization plans to produce the best products at the best cost and in the process achieve exceptional customer satisfaction. Windows into the soul of leadership, however, must be protected and remain confidential. The SWEATT model in the hands of a competitor becomes a distinct advantage for the competition – prudent communication is

Quality

required that demonstrates direction and pending actions but does not fully provide details which could be considered organizationally private.

Quality

The **final (and tenth) step** of the SWEATT process is repeating the SWEATT process. The SWEATT process, like the Wisdom to Tradition model, finds its value in the repetition of the process. Year over year, as the SWEATT process matures the strategic planning of the organization will improve – and the combination of the SWEATT models will provide a history of the strategic thinking of the organization.

SWEATT is a tool that is best used by leadership that is serious about improvement and change; with knowledge of the Wisdom to Tradition model (SWEATT naturally fits into the strategy, action and accountability sections of the Wisdom to Tradition model). SWEATT works when there is a passion for linking good ideas with metrics that are specific and for which the organization holds itself accountable. SWEATT is not for the meek or weak; SWEATT is for those organizations that can handle the tremendous honesty, courage and compassion it takes to develop and implement a model that focuses more on the stakeholders of the organization (investors, customers, suppliers, et al) than on the individual biases and territorial tendencies of organizational leaders. SWEATT, quite simply, is about change – change that is eventually reflected in the traditions of the organization.

SECTION II

LEADERSHIP

Defining
Quality

The most naïve hang onto the concept that the quality is what the customer says it is; that the customer defines quality. If this were true, and thank goodness it is not, unemployment would be high, employee motivation would be at an all-time low, organizations would fail and quality would be at its lowest ebb. Attempting to reason and do business in such an environment is bad for all involved. This chapter is about breaking the cycle of naïve thought and, once and for all, defining quality in a manner that the organizations that produce and provide products and services can thrive; in the process serving the correct customers who desire both value from the products and services they purchase and the ongoing financial health of the organizations that provide the products and services. The definition of quality must be managed carefully by organizations; establishing fair and consistent requirements that drive a competitive advantage for the organization and value for the correct customer. There is a lot in this view of quality - quality is a managed concept, the definition of quality is developed by the organization in such a manner to bring a competitive advantage and there are the correct and incorrect customers and stakeholders – let's dig deep into each area – starting with debunking three quality myths.

Myth #1: In the classic view, a customer is the individual that chooses to purchase a product or service from an organization. I view customers differently. To me, it is the organization that gets to decide who its customers are; a decision that must be taken seriously and strategically if the organization is to thrive and survive.

I call the customers selected by the organization correct customers. Customers who do not meet the criteria the organization establishes as acceptable must be discouraged and, in some cases, prohibited from purchasing the organization's products or services. An example of this concept is very selective universities. Universities exclude from their population students who do not meet their entrance requirements; even though there are many students who would gladly pay to attend the university yet who have not met the entrance requirements that the university has established. The correct customer, in the above example, is the prospective student who meets the entrance requirements of the university. The incorrect customer, in the above example, is the student who does not meet the entrance requirements of the university yet still desires to be part of the university's student body.

Even with the correct customers, however, there is a delicate relationship balance between the organization and the correct customer; a marriage so to speak. If one partner in the

Quality

relationship is unduly uncooperative, the relationship will eventually fail. The correct customer, as important as they are, needs to understand that without the organization being there to provide the products and services, there will be less of an opportunity for the correct customer to attain the product or service they desire. The correct customer must be a cooperative partner with the organization; otherwise damage will be done to both the organization (e.g. through reduced organizational value) and the correct customer (e.g. through the delivery of an unacceptable product or service or the non-delivery of the product or service entirely).

So, how does an organization select the customer types that will add value to the organization and, from there, direct the limited and valuable resources to the organization towards meeting the goals of those correct customers? Price is an easy way to self-select customer types; other ways are the location and hours of operation, the convenience or lack of convenience for the customer to purchase the product or service, use of regulations and laws that apply to the product or service, the compliance of the customer to regulations and laws (such as having a good driving record as a requirement for car insurance), the established mores of the community in which the product or service exists, the physical characteristics of the product; such as size and weight, the installation and service requirements of the product (e.g. the complexity of installation and the process for receiving service), the health of the customer (such as the disclosure of a pre-existing medical condition when applying for life insurance) or even, perhaps, the intelligence of the customer (such as in the student – university example cited earlier in this chapter).

Customers also need to help organizations understand their value; it is possible that a correct customer exists and that the organization does not know. In such cases, the correct customer must let the organization know of their existence. It would be best is an organization knew their own correct customer base; if not correct customers typically care enough to let the organization know who they are. For example, each year I let those firms with whom I do significant business, such as my dry cleaners, know the amount of money I have spent during the year with their organization – just to make sure they understand the relative value of my business and, when needed, so that they will make an exception to rush my orders outside their stated completion dates for dry cleaning. Correct customers do not like inconvenience; correct customers do not want to leave an organization; correct customers just want organizations they deal with to recognize them as correct customers and act appropriately. Appropriate actions relative to correct customers are simple:

---

1. they want the promises of the organization to be kept, and

2. they want to be treated better than the incorrect customers.

Stakeholders, on the other hand, have no direct financial investment in the organization; yet some stakeholders seem to believe that organizations have some level of accountability to them. Certainly, stakeholders are impacted by the actions of the organization; but unless the organization benefits from the stakeholder relationship there is really very little the organization must do to satisfy stakeholder requirements. Stakeholders who have influence on the organization's correct customers are known as correct stakeholders. Stakeholders who do not have an influence on the organization's correct customers are known as, at best, incorrect stakeholders and, at worst, worthless inconveniences. The struggle becomes, then, knowing which stakeholders really matter. With so many stakeholders this can be a difficult. The best way to define the correct stakeholders is to start with a control group; the correct customers. Having identified the correct customers, organizations can determine which stakeholders actually have significant influence on the correct customer base. The significant influencers of the correct customers will be the correct stakeholders of the organization.

Is it any wonder that organizations have difficulty defining quality when organizations base their definition of quality around a commingled group of correct customers and incorrect customers? It is time that we, as business leaders, take charge of how quality is defined, that we develop ways to select and manage the expectations of the correct customers and the correct stakeholders. Using this approach, organizations can achieve a common definition of quality that spans across products, services and organizational processes; one that extends to how organizational strategy is developed and implemented. By doing all this, organizations can create a correct customer base that is loyal, understanding, and respectful; a group that is willing to spend their money on the products and services the organizations provides for a very long time to come.

Quality

<u>Myth #2</u>: Another quality myth is that quality is the responsibility of everyone in the organization. The fallacy in this quality myth is that everyone in the organization has the education, experience, training and talent to manage the quality systems and processes of an organization. Would we expect everyone in the organization to be responsible for the marketing and sales function; of course not! Quality is a profession, not an endeavor. Quality requires expertise; quality does not just happen because of good intentions. Quality is full time job. When organizations embed in itself the idea that quality is so fundamental that a quality function is not necessary (e.g. the reliance on the six sigma concept), they have, in essence, created an environment where quality does not exist. For quality to become a competitive advantage:

1. the quality systems and processes of the organization must be led by a quality function that is self-sustaining,
2. that has the proper financial and human resources,
3. that has a high level of expertise, and
4. that has a direct line of accountability to the goals of the organization

Quality

Saying that quality is everyone's responsibility is just another way of saying quality is no one's responsibility; saying quality is everyone's responsibility is just another way of saying it is only a matter of time until the "for sale" sign is placed in  the front yard of the organization.

Quality

Myth 3: Now, the quality of the organization's products, services and processes are important – but perfection is not the quality standard. Quality professionals can lose sight of this simple tenet. Quality exists to help the organization succeed; quality is a journey, not a race – compromise is essential when those in quality are dealing with other parts of the organization. It is critical to remember that organizations have and will continue to exist without a quality department; quality departments, however, cannot exist without the organization. Quality professionals need humility; they may hold the keys to the release of new designs and innovation but this power must be used only when absolutely necessary. A quality organization full of egotistical and power hungry individuals is a recipe for disaster; for the organization, for the quality profession and for the correct customers and the correct stakeholders. In my career as a quality professional I cannot think of one instance where I had to act in a manner, on a significant event, that was not supported by the organization. Quality professionals use their professional expertise and judgment to help others understand the rules and regulations of quality and the logic of quality based decisions. Just as marketing individuals use their skills to help others understand marketing, quality professionals do the same related to quality. It is critical to remember that, with all decisions (quality included), that decisions affect humans – and humans need to believe they have been fairly heard before they will accept the outcome of any decision. Listen –

be fair – act in the best interest of the investors – and all will go well.

Three critical concepts from the discussion of the three myths:

1. organizations get to select their own customers,

2. there must be quality professionals embedded within the organization, and

3. those in quality must act with humility.

Now, let's move on to the traits of quality. We will examine each trait and how the traits link to how an organization defines quality.

Quality

Traits of Quality

There are five general traits of quality, those being:

1. Belief

2. Compliance

3. Regulatory

4. Unreasonable

5. Value

Quality

Belief: We all start out using the belief trait of quality; for some products and services we never outgrow this trait. The belief trait is emotion based, quality is perceived as either good or bad based upon an experience with the product or service or what has been heard or written about the product or service. The belief trait of quality is based on antidotes; correct customers that use the belief trait are hard to gain, hard to lose, and hard to regain. Using the belief trait, correct customers will suffer through poor quality for a long time before ceasing to purchase a product or service elsewhere. Conversely, once an unfavorable impression prevails, the correct customers will take a very long time to become purchasers again as the trust bond between the organization and the correct customers will have been damaged. We all use the belief trait to some extent; either through prioritization or through laziness. Relative to prioritization, the correct customers may or may not have the time to do an extensive analysis of product or service quality, so the belief trait prevails. Using the prioritization approach, the types of products or services that would fit into the belief trait would be those products or services which do not have a significant impact on the correct customers. Using the laziness approach, all products and services fit into the belief trait. The laziness approach, relative to the correct customers, does not involve data as a decision making tool, so no amount of new independent data will affect the correct customer's decision to purchase or not to purchase in the short term; the decision to purchase is based on some amount of bias by the correct customer towards the product or service. It is critical for organizations to understand, relative to the belief trait of quality, that retained correct customers may not be a good indication of customer satisfaction

Quality

Compliance: This is the type of quality trait that is accepted by the correct customer as being accurate, precise and measurable; where products and services are defined by their consistency and their conformance to requirements. Correct customers that define quality by this trait expect products and services to have little, if any, variation in performance. Correct customers who use this trait to judge quality may or may not know what the proper specifications for a product or service, but they are able to detect variations in products and services. An example of the use of the compliance trait would be an automobile; there is an expectation that the automobile will perform consistently for a long period of time; correct customers may not know the specifications under which the automobile was built yet they are still astute enough to know when there is a problem with the car well before the warning indicator light illuminates.

Quality

Regulatory: This is the type of quality trait that is legislated by governments, standard bodies, and professional associations. The regulatory trait is the price of market entry for an organization; yet the regulatory trait may or may not offer a competitive advantage for the organization. The correct customer uses the regulatory trait from the view of the lack of compliance, rather than compliance.

For example, if an organization is mandated to recall a product the correct customer will use the regulatory trait to judge the overall totality of quality of other products manufactured by the  organization, but not yet recalled. In essence, the failure of one product will indicate to the correct customer the potential for other products to be defective – even if the other products of the organization meet all applicable regulations.

Quality

Unreasonable: This is the type of quality trait where the correct customer judges the product or service quality using their own standard of quality, often perfection. The correct customer, in this trait, creates more pain than value to the organization; creating dissatisfaction for themselves and for the organization. If the unreasonable trait is allowed to exist, the organization will eventually fail.

Quality

Value: The value trait is used by the correct customer in their determination of the acceptable price for a product or service. Correct customers use the value trait to understand that two products or services, priced differently, can have the same level of quality. For example, purchasing a first class ticket on an airplane offers seats that are wider and more comfortable than a coach class ticket. The value trait demonstrates that the expectation of comfort and service will be less for the coach environment as opposed to the first class environment, yet both environments are equal in quality (i.e. the expectations of each correct customer has been met; in this case there are actually two distinct correct customer populations) normalized by the price that each correct customer has paid for their ticket. Influence of the unreasonable trait impacts the value trait as the organization will never be  able to satisfy the correct customer base if the unreasonable trait is present. In the above example, the unreasonable trait would lead the correct customer to expect the same type of service and comfort in both coach and first class.

Quality

Characteristics of Quality

The traits of quality form the base for how quality is defined. Although there are many ways to define the characteristics of product and service quality, I have simplified the process so that one set of characteristics apply to both products and services. This is a radical and new approach to defining the characteristics of quality. The specific characteristics of product and service quality can be viewed in a diagram I call the quality characteristic circle.

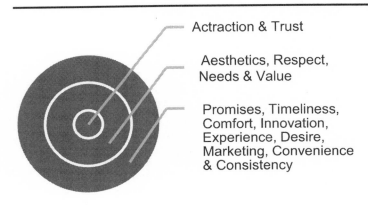

Actraction & Trust

Aesthetics, Respect, Needs & Value

Promises, Timeliness, Comfort, Innovation, Experience, Desire, Marketing, Convenience & Consistency

The quality characteristic circle contains three rings with a series of outside influences. The inner core of the quality characteristic circle contains the elements of attraction and trust. The secondary circle of the quality characteristic circle contains the elements aesthetics, respect, needs and value. The outer circle of the quality characteristic circle contains the elements of stated promises, implied promises, timeliness, comfort, innovation, before, during and after experience, desire, marketing, convenience and consistency.

The forces acting on the quality characteristic circle are the correct and incorrect customer base and the correct and incorrect stakeholder base.

Quality

Elements of the **inner** core are:

1. <u>Attraction</u> may be the look of the product, the look of the service personnel (e.g. appearance, demeanor or professionalism of dress), the perceived glamour of the organization (e.g. working with a television network sounds exciting) or the appearance of the environment in which the product and or service is to be provided (e.g. marble floors in the organizational headquarters). Organizations must accept that having a good personality is not enough; to succeed organizations must have the total package; brains, personality and a look that is pleasing to the eye. Think about how people select mates; the first impression makes a big difference!

2. Only after attraction has been achieved, then <u>trust</u> becomes a consideration. If a correct customer or correct stakeholder does not trust the organization to provide safe, usable, and functional products and services or does not trust the organization to act within applicable laws and regulations or does not trust the organization to live up to its explicit and implicit promises the other quality characteristics will not matter. Attraction and trust are the price of market entry relative to product and service quality.

Quality

The **secondary** circle contains the elements of aesthetics, respect, needs and value.

1. <u>Aesthetics</u> is defined as a subjective assessment of product and service quality; e.g. the color or feel of a product. I contend that aesthetics is a very objective measure of product and service quality, aesthetics can be used to establish the expectation level of correct customer; aesthetics can provide the competitive identity for the product or service. Aesthetics is different from attraction in that aesthetics is more permanent; attraction is based on the emotional first impression of a product or service whereas aesthetics is based on the longer lasting aspects of a product or service. Aesthetics is a non-functional aspect of a product or service, aesthetics directly affects how the correct customer will perceive how the product will perform or how the service will be delivered, which in turn affects the value of the product or service. The look of an organization, the décor and color scheme, the outlay of the processes all are aesthetics that impact perception of an organization's product and service quality.

2. <u>Respect</u> is how the correct customers are treated by the personal that provide or support the product or provide the

service; this includes everyone in the product and service chain. Respect, in the secondary circle, deals with an expectation of minimal respect. Respect is much more than being polite, though being polite is an expectation. Given that the organization meets the minimum standard of politeness, the concept of respect expands to the length of time devoted (e.g. the time a doctor takes to listen to a patient prior to interrupting) and the expertise level of the organization's personnel. Respect

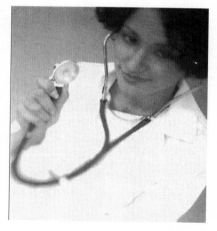

is a base line requirement that will not necessarily be rewarded with sales, revenue and reputation; however the lack of respect is a path towards the loss of sales, revenue and reputation.

3. <u>Needs</u>, in the secondary circle, is much different from desires. A need is just that, a need. For example, a need for a business traveler relative to a hotel room would include such items as cleanliness, safety, location, wireless internet, a comfortable and efficient work desk and accurate billing. It is critical that the correct customer and the correct customer understand the

difference between a need and a desire. If the concept of need and desire are commingled, there may be confusion between the concepts of expected quality and exceptional quality; the latter being the quality level used by the organization to separate itself from the competition.

4. <u>Value</u> is the output of the inner circle (attraction and trust) and the secondary circle characteristics of aesthetics, respect and needs. The correct customer will decide if the value of the product or service is consistent with the price charged for the product or service. If the correct customer deems the price to match the value, the outer circle elements will become important; if not the third circle elements never come into play.

Quality

The **outer** circle of the quality characteristic circle contains the characteristics of stated promises, implied promises, timeliness, comfort, innovation, before, during and after experience, desires, marketing, convenience and consistency.

1. <u>Stated promises</u> are those promises that the organization directly makes; the correct customer expects the organization to keep its stated promises 100% of the time. Organizations need to think long and hard before making a stated promise. Examples of stated promises would include warranties, service with a smile or the promise that orders will be processed within 24 hours of receipt.

2. <u>Implied promises</u> are those promises the correct customers believe the organization makes without the organization actually having made the promise. Organizations must work diligently to constrain the interpretation of an implied promise. Examples of an implied promise would be allowing the return of a product without a receipt (given the organization has a customer satisfaction policy that uses such wording as "we will always make our customers happy" or "customer satisfaction is our only purpose").

Quality

3. <u>Timeliness</u> is the time it takes to acquire a product or receive a service. Correct customers have their own view of timeliness; the organization can help define timeliness by posting policies regarding timeliness; e.g. by posting that fast food meals will be delivered in less than 3 minutes or that no check-out lines at a retail store will exceed 5 customers in line.

4. <u>Comfort</u> is the expectation of correct customer and correct stakeholder to feel welcome and comfortable during the product performance or service delivery. For example, the layout of a retail store may have the feeling of being packed into the store or, conversely, that they have ample room to maintain some private and thinking space, the intensity of the lighting may affect how someone experiences a dinner at a restaurant.

5. <u>Innovation</u> is the part of product performance or the delivery of a service that substantially adds value. Innovation is not about slow continuous improvement or minor changes in a product or service. Innovation, though not expected in every product or service encounter, is a frequent expectation in the life cycle of the product or service. The innovation of a product or service is not something that the correct customer may be able to identify themself. Innovation is about the using the resources of the

organization to find ways to help the correct customer view the product and service changes as dramatic and exciting.

6. The next element in the quality characteristic circle is the before, during and after experience. The correct customer more than likely have been exposed to the product or service before they actually use the product or experience the service. The organization must manage the exposure of the product and service; this might include product or service testimonials or even trial samples of the product. The next step is for the correct customer to actually use the product or experience the service; this is where the organization must assure the product or service is used or experienced within the boundaries the organization has set for the product or service. The after experience is the most critical part of the experience cycle; this is where the correct customers change their needs relative to the product or service. For example, the first time we experience a ride on a motorcycle we might have a primary need of safety; the second time the need of performance is added. Organizations must anticipate the after experience requirements and provide them in the product or service design.

7. Desire is the quality characteristic that the organization must find a way to get the correct customer to pay more for; either in

money, word of mouth advertising, influence or long-term loyalty. Organizations will not be able to fulfill every desire; nor would the correct customer be able to afford every desire they have for a product or service. When an organization chooses to fulfill a desire of the correct customer this must be strategic decision based upon customer value.

8. <u>Marketing</u> may seem an odd quality characteristic; however marketing plays a significant role in how the other quality characteristics are viewed. Marketing impacts the stated and implied promises relative to the product or service, marketing impacts the attraction of the product or service and marketing impacts the aesthetics of the product or service. The quality of the marketing effort for a product or service can be linked to how the product or service quality is perceived before, during and after use of the product or service. This can be as simple as the correct customer believing that if an organization believes in the product or service enough to launch a professional marketing campaign then the product or service is worth the try; conversely if all the organization can do is muster a black and white newspaper advertisement buried deep in the local happenings section of a newspaper the correct customer may not feel as compelled to purchase the product or service.

9. <u>Convenience</u> is the amount of effort it takes to purchase the product or service; this can be locational or process oriented. For example the ability to do personal banking at one of many locations, using an ATM card or online is a convenience characteristic of banking.

10. <u>Consistency</u> involves the amount of variation in a product performance or service delivery that the correct customer is willing to tolerate. The correct customer thrives on consistency; very few of us like unpleasant surprises. Examples of consistency would include receiving the same haircut every time you go to the salon, going to the grocery store and finding the items each week in the same location or having online banking systems that have the same formats and operational features. Consistency is not about the lack of change; consistency is about planned change.

Quality

Factors Pushing on the Circle

The factors which push and pull on the quality characteristics circle are the influence of the correct customer base, the influence of the incorrect customer base, the influence of the correct stakeholder base and the influence of the incorrect stakeholder base. The quality characteristic circle is based on paying attention to the correct customer and correct stakeholder base only, which is why I have ignored the incorrect customer base and the incorrect stakeholder base in the discussion of the elements of the quality characteristics circle. Ignoring the incorrect customer and the incorrect stakeholders, however, does not make these groups disappear – which is why I continue to list them as having influence. It takes time, but if the incorrect customers and the incorrect stakeholders are ignored long enough their influence will become less and less – but never zero – pests rarely leave – they just get to the point that they are no longer visible.

The quality characteristics circle is not an easy process to understand or implement; but it is well worth the effort. When we overlay the traits of quality on the quality characteristics circle, we can begin to see how an organization can actually define quality for their correct customer and correct stakeholder base.

Requirement	Trait	Inner Core	Secondary Circle	Outer Core
Lawnmower Starts on First Pull	Belief – The more recognizable the brand name the better Compliance – I expect the mower to operate consistently Regulatory – I expect the lawnmower to be safe Value – I expect the have options available with respect to cost and features	The lawnmower must look "cool"; there must be a trust factor that the lawnmower company knows how to manufacturer a lawnmower	There must be mulch capability; a catch bag is not needed. The lawnmower must fit within a budget. When the lawnmower is purchased there will be an expectation of advice offered by store personnel.	The lawnmower should be easy to assemble and perform as expected; there must be some neat new gadgets associated with the lawnmower, the lawnmower must be agronomical et al.

Quality

Yet, sometimes the correct customers and the correct stakeholders can still be harmful. In my dissertation work, I found an interesting link between what a customer tells an organization and how they actually act – the two being opposites of each other. I asked there different groups: the purchaser of the product or service, the user of a product or service and professionals in the quality field to describe, using classic quality elements, how they valued quality in a product or service. From there, I asked each group to describe their own customer satisfaction with specific products and services and examined their spending patterns with each specific product or service. Then, given the data, I used a multiple regression model to determine, based upon what each group espoused, which would be the products or services highest and lowest in customer satisfaction and highest and lowest in products and services produced. Interestingly, for groups one and two (the purchasers and the users) the results were inverse to the regression models – e.g. the elements of quality most valued by the group were, in reality, the worst for the products or services that the groups rated the best quality. In essence, the customer groups said one thing and then acted just the opposite. Well, either the groups lied – e.g. stating that reliability was the #1 purchase criteria for a car when in reality their #1 criteria was aesthetics – or there are elements of the quality that have not yet been identified. There may be a few elements of quality yet to be uncovered – but in this case it is much more likely that the groups were not honest - what the correct customer believed to be true and the way they acted was not in step with the way they judged quality or spent their money. The third group (the quality professionals), however, did not have this problem – in their case this group espoused preferences that were supported by the regression models.

So, what does this tell us – well, if our correct customers truly understand our products at a deep technical level we may be able to draw some important and useful information from the group as we seek to define quality for a product or service – but if the correct customer does not have a deep technical understanding of a product or service then the information we gather may be harmful and false – leading to incorrect definitions of quality.

Wow – lots of information and thoughts on the role of quality in an organization, the traits and characteristics of quality and how the correct customers can provide (sometimes) misleading and harmful information to organizations. How does all this fit into one elegant definition of quality?

Quality

Here is how I would define the concept of quality and how I would define quality:

Quality is achieved through the application of organizational knowledge; through the development of and delivery on a defined set of requirements that achieve value for both the correct customers and the correct stakeholders and the organization. Quality is what the organization defines it to be given a structure of extensive research and analysis under the premise of increasing stockholder value; which then translates into what the correct customer and the correct stakeholder finds of value.

Dr. Russell Roberson

Quality

It took a long time to get to the definition; but the definition makes sense when viewed in context of the three myths of quality, the traits of quality, the characteristics of quality and the potential for misleading and damaging information being provided through the correct customer base.   In this definition the traits of belief, compliance, regulatory, unrealistic and value are all covered and place the responsibility for defining quality squarely on the organization.   This is a radical shift from the concept that the customer defines quality and that the customer is always right; a shift that is long, long overdue!

Quality

The Characteristics of an Executive Leader

Being part of the executive management team in an organization is tough. To help guide myself on my own quality journey, I developed a list of expectations; a list I now call "Ten Characteristics of an Executive Leader". I have shared this list across many organizations; from those just beginning their careers in quality to the most seasoned executives. The key to the top ten list is in understanding that quality has a unique role in an organization – starting with oversight that assures the organization complies with applicable laws and regulations and ending with playing a significant part of product, process and service improvements which help organizations achieve a competitive advantage.

Leadership is more than making decisions; leadership is about knowing the capabilities of the ship and the crew first, then steering the ship into the correct port of call.

Quality

A QUALITY LEADER:

1. must never lose sight that quality is part of the organization; quality is not the sole reason for the organization to exist

2. must establish a quality system that the organization can understand and implement

3. must understand the rules that govern how the organization must behave

4. must know the products and services that the organization provides; both their use and misuse

5. must not make decisions on over-simplified information

6. must take proper actions in a timely manner

7. gets other leaders to be an active part of the quality systems of the organization

8. must look for signs of change in the organization before the organization experiences the change; then takes the necessary actions to prevent any unwanted anticipated change from damaging the organization

9. understands the organization's quality intelligence and maturity and the relative impact on the quality systems of the organization

10. establishes quality as a career growth path in the organization

Quality

Leadership Tenet 1:   A quality leader must never lose sight that quality is part of the organization; quality is not the sole reason for the organization to exist. This is a critical first point; positioned #1 in the list to drive home that quality organization must not overstate their worth to the organization and the organizational stakeholders. The quality organization exists at the pleasure of the organization; not vice – versa. A tenet I use to support point #1 is that "quality is not in the business of putting the business out of business". The quality organization must look at quality initiatives and quality based decisions from a risk – reward perspective. There are very few binary decisions in the field of quality; it is the responsibility of the quality organization to actively look for ways to help the organization succeed. An example of this might be when a decision must be made regarding a potential product recall. It is my contention that a well-run quality organization starts with the position of not wanting to recall the product (even though the quality organization might have the authority to initiate such a recall) and moves, at a proper pace with the proper information, towards the last resort of a product recall action.   Taking this approach demonstrates to the organization that the quality organization, seeking to fully comply with applicable laws and regulations, does not leap first to the most conservative action. When actions such as recall must happen, the

Quality

organization can rest assured that all possible alternatives prior to making the recall decision have been examined and vetted. When quality leaders lose perspective on their relative importance within the organization, they soon lose credibility – from there the loss of influence follows – with the loss of influence the quality leader becomes ineffective.

Quality

Leadership Tenet 2: A quality leader must establish a quality system that the organization can understand and implement. This point links to the Wisdom to Tradition model; where multiple cycles of the Wisdom to Tradition model may be required to achieve the changes in processes and culture desired by the leadership of the organization. Change, to be accepted and implemented well, must match the capability of the organization. A quality leader has to understand this concept at a deep level; being able to compromise on what parts of a quality system can be implemented over time and which parts of a quality system must be implemented without compromise. For example, honesty regarding records and documents would be an element of the quality system in which no compromise is possible; immediate compliance to this part of the quality system would be required. However, there are parts of the quality system that could be allowed to grow and mature over time; e.g. the development and implementation of a product testing process that examines atypical workflows might be a quality system where incremental change over time would produce results that are robust in nature, well-understood and seen as necessary by those who do the work.

Leadership Tenet 3: A quality leader must understand the rules that govern how the organization must behave. If you did not know the general tax laws, imagine how nervous you would be each year when you filed your taxes. The same holds true for quality leaders. For an individual to be an effective part of the quality system they reside within, they must have read, understood, and implemented the laws and regulations that affect the organizational products, services and processes to the letter; ignorance by a quality leader relative to the applicable laws and regulations is disservice to the organization who depends on the quality leader to provide the legal compass. It is not possible to know if laws and regulations are being broken, or bent, unless the laws and regulations are known and understood. This tenet is well supported by maturity and experience, where knowledge of laws and regulations are often best absorbed over time through work in the area of quality. It is the responsibility of the quality leader to assure the rules under which the organization must operate are clearly understood by the correct customers and the correct stakeholders (e.g. employees, suppliers et al).

Quality

Leadership Tenet 4: A quality leader must know the products and services the organization provides; both their use and misuse. In order to be effective, a quality leader must understand both the science and the workflow of the products and services provided by the organization. This extends to include the processes used by the organization to produce and deliver the products and services aforementioned. Understanding the science of a product and service means understanding theory – i.e. why does the product work or why does the service meet the needs of the customer. An example of this in my field is understanding the science behind how a medical drug or medical device works – understanding the chemistry of the human body as linked to the science of the medical drug or device. Another example, relative to my field, would be in seeking an understanding of how software coding is performed. In such a case, training specific to the skill of software coding would be appropriate in addition to an understanding of how the product is used. Understanding the science allows the quality leader to make informed decisions regarding appropriate metrics, data analysis and the like. Understanding workflow is the process of understanding how the product or service is used properly, as intended. Understanding workflow involves the inherent understanding of the user and any inconvenience to the user that may be caused by the

Quality

designed workflows. It is not enough, however, to understand the organizational products and services at a scientific and workflow level – a quality leader must also understand how the products and services of the organization might be misused. Misuse has many methods; most unintentional and some intentional –misuse is rarely intended to create an unsafe condition for the user or for the those that are affected by the organization's products and services. Understanding misuse conditions the quality leader can steer the quality systems of the organization such that reasonable misuse conditions are known and accounted for; either through design, use instructions or mitigation (e.g. fail safe conditions designed into a product). Understanding misuse not only allows the organization to protect the user of the product and service; misuse information can also act as feed data into the design processes of the organization – which may lead to even more innovative designs that satisfy the need of the user.

Quality

Leadership Tenet 5: The quality leader must not make decisions on over-simplified information. It might just be me, but I strongly believe that in order to improve a product, service or process there must be a deep understanding of the product, service or process. As such, an effective quality leader not only understands the importance of detail but also understands the process of analysis; specifically the statistical tools used to gather and analyze data. Any individual who desires a successful career in the quality profession would do themself well to master the concept of statistics (at the graduate level). This would include a deep understanding of the concepts of study design, sampling, confidence intervals, hypothesis testing, level of significance, regressions, analysis of variance, chi-square, type 1 and type 2 errors and the like. It cannot be overstated the importance of a quality leader having a grasp of the statistical tools used when making quality based decisions. Now, this does not mean that there is not a constructive use for the "red-yellow-green" (RYG) systems seen in so many quality reviews. RYG systems work well – as long as those who use the RYG process understand how the RYG indicators were determined. It is the responsibility of an effective quality leader to make decisions on holistic information that has been collected properly and analyzed correctly.

Leadership Tenet 6: A quality leader must take proper actions in a timely manner. Quality leaders, typically, have the authority and responsibility to take actions in a timely manner – to assure the success of the organization and the safety of the users of the organization's products and services. For a quality leader, the decision timeline does not start when they knew about something, but instead when the organization knew about something or when the organization should have known about something. As such, an effective quality leader must implement a quality system that brings forth information in a timely manner – timely actions are not possible without timely information. The definition of timely can certainly be debated; the quality leader must have a set of decision criteria that guides when a decision must be made. For example, relative to a product recall decision the quality leader may establish a set of information required to make the recall decision – or given the information is not available by a set time make the decision siding towards the recall. It has been my experience that timeliness is defined significantly different by the quality leader and the general public. I think the reason for this is the misunderstanding by the general public on the impact of the recall decision. The decision to recall a product is delicate balancing act – act too quickly and recall the product and users are inconvenienced, supply chains are interrupted and the reputation of the organization may be damaged – all for a problem that may not even exist (this would be a type 1 error). For products such as in my field, recalling a product could actually cause great harm to those users whom the recall would not affect (e.g. a medical side effect not typically experienced by the general public relative to a medical drug). Waiting too long to recall a product potentially endangers the user (this would be a type 2 error); this option is obviously not the desired choice. Given the two sides of the recall decision, an effective quality leader must make the prudent decision – which from an organizational and general public view should be after the appropriate information has been gathered and analyzed. It should not be surprising, then, that decisions of this magnitude take time and patience – when made they are not reversible. Taking three – four months to understand a situation and then make a decision would, in most cases, seem timely – however to the general public this might seem as if the organization was not acting properly. The difference of opinion, in my view, is in the lack of understanding of the general public relative to the impact of the recall decision on those other than the user – that and my belief that a good percentage of the public has an inherent bias towards believing organizations will desire profit over safety. This is actually opposite of reality – organizations would be

Quality

the first to make a recall decision – delaying such a decision too

long only exposes the organization to litigation, fines and a loss of

reputation.   Timely is a difficult measure to meet – an effective

quality leader is able to tread this trail properly by using established

metrics and decision criteria.

Quality

Leadership Tenet 7: A quality leader gets other leaders to be an active part of the quality systems of the organization. This sounds easy, but it can be very difficult to achieve. Being an active part of the quality system is not just showing up at a few meetings and speaking on the importance of quality. This type of limited activity is a far way from being an active part of the quality system process. To be an active part of the quality system process requires organizational leaders to have specific goals and objectives that:

1. link to quality system compliance and hold the organizational leader accountable for non-compliance to the quality system,

2. encourage the best and brightest to be part of the quality team during some part of their career,

3. look upon customer visits not only as a sales opportunity but also to understand how the organization's products and services are being used

4. take responsibility for the robustness of the organization's quality systems, and

5. prevent organizational leaders from approving records and documents when the established requirements have not been met.

Quality

Just at it takes time for an organization to mature over time relative to the implementation of a quality system; it will take time for the leadership of the organization to fully embed in their goals and objectives full support of the quality systems. However, the patience for change relative to the leadership of the organization should be short (as compared to the patience for change relative to the holistic organization). Leadership that does not get on board relative to the support of the quality system must be identified by the quality leader and additional efforts and time must be spent with this type of individual to help with an understanding of the importance of the total leadership support of the quality systems of the organization. In the best case, leadership gets "it" and becomes fully supportive of the quality systems of the organization; in the worst case some of the leadership of the organization may need to exit the organization.

Leadership Tenet 8: A quality leader must look for signs of change in the organization before the organization experiences the change; then takes the necessary actions to prevent any unwanted anticipated change from damaging the organization. This tenet requires not only an inquisitive mind, but deep metric development, data analysis and statistical skills as well. This skill set crosses the boundaries of the qualitative and quantitative areas; from understanding changes needed in strategy and talent to changes needed in product and service design. Taking the time to put in place indicators of quality and predictors of performance is critical; then taking the time to look for the relevant messages is mandatory if the quality leader is going to be able to detect the signs of pending change. This requires looking at data and situations from many different views, looking not only at data and information as presented but also at what data and information is missing. In some cases this may require making assumptions or even speculating regarding a situation; all to better understand the past and present so as to have a reasonable chance at predicting the future. A dedication of time, on a very routine basis, with the patience to ponder in deep thought is the only way I know how to achieve this tenet. Then, when the quality leader believes they have detected a sign of change, there must be a structured and well designed test to minimize the probability of any action resulting in a type 1 error (i.e. taking an action when no action is needed). Quality leaders live in type 2 error daily (i.e. failing to take an action when an action is needed) and such is the case when signs of change go unrecognized. So – in the case of tenet #8, the risk is in over reacting and acting when there is not a need to act; which only serves to cause disruption to the organizational processes. Such a test will help the quality leader understand the probability of the change and from there a decision can be made on the type 1 and type 2 risks. Then again, sometimes intuitive skills, after all is said and done can become the deciding factor – this may sound a bit dangerous but with the properly seasoned quality leader the mix of intuition and experimentation is often the combination that works the best.

Quality

Leadership Tenet 9: A quality leader understands the organization's quality intelligence and maturity and the relative impact on the quality systems of the organization. Before quality leader can adapt to the organization intelligence and maturity, they would need to be able to identify the stages of organizational intelligence and maturity. I have developed a five stage model that examines critical elements of organizational intelligence and maturity as directly related to the quality systems of an organization. In my model, the five stages of organizational maturity are:

1. Denial – this is the stage of ignorant bliss, the organization has no idea just how bad things are and how much worse things are eventually to become; this is the stage of egotistical behavior

2. Anger – this is the stage where the organization starts to understand change is necessary, at a deep level; yet change is resisted hoping that with enough resistance to change that the idea of change will vanish; this is the state of abusive behavior

3. Acceptance – this is the stage where the organization gives up on trying to stop change and reluctantly accepts that change must happen; this is the state of recognition

4. Competitive – this is the stage where the organization realizes the potential for significant bottom line improvement given an effective quality system; along with an understanding of the

amount of work that would be needed to accomplish such; this is the state of dedication

5. Elegance – the simplest solutions are the most elegant solutions; this is where the organization gains a laser like focus on which parts of the quality systems of the organization to invest in and which parts of the quality systems of the organization not to invest in; this is the state of sustainment and simplicity.

In the pages to follow, I have provided a listing of characteristics that indicate the intelligence and maturity level of an organization (relative to the organization's quality systems). This chart can be used to determine the quality maturity stage of an organization and the pace of change relative to quality system improvements. Change in organizations must be planned, executed and verified; only is it appropriate to move to the next stage of change. In my model, this would imply that movement within the model must follow the path of stages; i.e. it is not possible to jump over a complete organizational stage and achieve success.

	Denial	Anger	Acceptance	Competitive	Elegance
Culture	Culture is seen as exemplary - with no need for change	The need for a culture change is recognized but is also resented	Understanding that culture must change; which may require a different type of employee	Culture reflects a deep respect for the investors	Culture reflects a deep respect for the investors and the correct customer
Customer Focus	Organization is overly reactive to customers; all customers are treated as equal	The need for a culture change is recognized but is also resented	Understanding that culture must change; which may require a different type of employee	Culture reflects a deep respect for the investors	Culture reflects a deep respect for the investors and the correct customer
Empowerment	Self-directed empowerment happens without organizational direction; very little awareness of change	The need for a culture change is recognized but is also resented	Understanding that culture must change; which may require a different type of employee	Culture reflects a deep respect for the investors	Culture reflects a deep respect for the investors and the correct customer

	Denial	Anger	Acceptance	Competitive	Elegance
Leadership Mentality	Understand the need to invest in quality yet fail to do so	The need for a culture change is recognized but is also resented	Understanding that culture must change; which may require a different type of employee	Culture reflects a deep respect for the investors	Culture reflects a deep respect for the investors and the correct customer
Leadership Message	Everything is ok; just keep the focus.	Everything is still ok; the customers and the market do not understand the strategy of the organization	There are problems which will required core changes to the quality systems of the organization	Any problems the organization faces will be resolved in a holistic manner	Most problems are prevented, those that are not get high management attention
Management of Change	Change happens to the organization without planning	Change is viewed as a weakness	Change processes are developed and change is accepted as necessary	Change is a strategic choice	Change is part of the organizational culture; change benefits both the correct customer and the investor

Quality

	Denial	Anger	Acceptance	Competitive	Elegance
Measurement	Quality indicators are measured for show only; information is not used to drive improvements	Measurement focus mostly on financial indicators; rare to see measurements focused on quality	Measurements, relative to quality, are utilized – but are mostly reactive in nature	Innovative thought begins relative to measurement; dedication to measurement is becoming part of the norm	Measurement drives the strategic decision making process
Process Control	Process are somewhat predictable and stable	Process becomes less predictable and less stable	Processes become predictable and stable	Process predictability and stability can be moved from process to process	Process consistency is seen by the correct customers and the correct stakeholders
Stakeholder Focus	Organization places little or no value on stakeholder relationships	Organization is a bully to stakeholders	Organization begins to segment stakeholders by correct and incorrect	Organization has a strategic focus on the correct stakeholder groups	The correct stakeholder group helps drive the organizational bottom line improvements

	Denial	Anger	Acceptance	Competitive	Elegance
Statistical Knowledge	Everyone in the organization believes they are a statistician; statistical models, used incorrectly.	Statistical information is used to justify the status quo	Organization recognizes the need for statistical knowledge and begins to hire statisticians	Basic statistical models are used; such as testing design, customer trials, et al	Advanced statistical models are used; such as testing design, customer trials, et al.
Supply Chain	Relationship with suppliers is driven by cost and delivery; suppliers are seen as replaceable.	Suppliers are blamed for problems; payment of suppliers is delayed thus affecting supplier cash	Suppliers are seen as critical to the organization; organization seeks to repair supplier relationships	Suppliers are managed by a formal process; change control is a critical component of supplier management	Supplier are part of the process of design, innovation and growth
Teamwork	Teams exist but there is no constructive conflict, teams are focused on non-strategic quality goals	Teams are seen as destructive; as taking too much time to reach decisions and then act in a proper manner	Organization gets the teamwork is critical to innovation and growth; begins to invest in team development	Teams are deployed to help organization achieve strategic objectives	Teams utilize the matrix process of accountability and drive bottom line improvements

Training	Denial	Anger	Acceptance	Competitive	Elegance
	Training is an afterthought; only done when all other ideas for investment are exhausted.	Training is seen as a necessary evil; investments in training are done because some higher up in the organization forces the training to happen.	Organization recognizes the need training and starts to develop an immediate and short-term training strategy. Training is conducted at the most basic levels – shoring up knowledge that should already be present in the organization but is not present.	Training has a strong technical focus; a long-term training strategy is developed. Training is driven by current and future talent competency models.	Training is part of the culture of the organization; training is used as a retention and attraction tool.

Quality

An effective quality leader is able to understand the (quality system) intelligence and maturity level of the organization in which they operate and adopt. This concept links to the Wisdom to Tradition model discussed in chapter #1 of this book; recall that multiple cycles of the Wisdom to Tradition model may be needed to achieve the desired organization changes. Understanding the five stages of organization (quality system) intelligence and maturity should help the leadership of the organization as they navigate through multiple Wisdom to Tradition cycles.

Quality

<u>Leadership Tenet 10</u>: A quality leader establishes quality as a career growth path in the organization. For an organization to succeed in the long – term, there must be a credo that the success of any career is determined, in part, on a reasonable tenure in the area of quality and compliance management. Management must groom its employees to see quality as a route along their career path, not a detour. As I have mentored others during my career, I am often asked about my career choices. My response to questions of this type is to discuss my leadership journey and encourage others to develop their own leadership journey charts. The elements of my leadership journey charts are quite simple – what was my role, what did I learn and how did I apply what I had learned. Reviewing this chart over the years has helped me mature as a leader. The leadership journey chart helps me provide advice and guidance that is meaningful and data based. You might note that I do not have a next position category in my leadership journey; this is on purpose. My belief is that if an individual manages their current positions well, then the next position in their leadership journey will seek them out rather than having to be sought out. This requires trust in the processes of the organization to recognize and reward talent and dedication by the individual to stay focused on the job at hand – rather than looking so far down the road they make a misstep in their current role.

Quality

Leadership Position	General Responsibility	What Did I Learn?	How Did I Apply What I Learned?
QARA VP	Responsible for QA / RA software and compliance; design / manufacturing / service for both medical devices and non-medical devices	Trust is given initially based on past performance; trust is retained based upon establishing clear expectations and delivering on those expectations.	Driving improvements across the business; CAPA, complaints, design, etc.
Director, Global Quality - Devices	Product and compliance quality for operations, design engineering and HQ; Medical Devices only; FDA et al interaction	Leaders need to learn the culture first, and then act. Simple goals work best Compliance is about continually improving	Improvements in core QMS elements Improve in staff quality skill set and maturity
Director, Global Quality – Devices and Drugs	Product and compliance quality for operations, design engineering and HQ; Medical Drugs and Devices only; FDA et al interaction Responsible for R&QE, CAPA, customer support	Process control is critical Sampling plans must be based on process history Customer interactions with quality improve product and service performance FDA reacts well to decision tress, timely investigations, and robust CAPA	Quality defects at all-time low Process control at all time high FDA inspections zero system failures Implemented customer service teams Implement defect early detection teams Organization produced leaders

Leadership Position	General Responsibility	What Did I Learn?	How Did I Apply What I Learned?
R&QE Manager	Managed R&QE, involved with FMEA, MMEA, HFA, supplier assessments, etc.	Prevention and mistake proofing are the two most useful quality tools	Reduced blood spills through new gasket design
Quality Manager	Managed quality operation for the a clinical device and prototype plant	Oversight is critical in low volume production	Developed prototype manufacturing line

Managed division warehouse |
| Corporate Quality Auditor | Performed GxP assessments of operations; provided training and troubleshooting operations on QMS and engineering; developed strategies for FDA inspections; performed supplier assessments; performed due diligence assessments. | Different is not necessarily wrong

Audits need to detect system problems

The way you say something matters

Audit reports need to be accurate and compassionate | Designed QMS for many different operations (e.g. implants, marketing, etc.)

Audit results prevented

FDA observations through earlier detection and correction |

Leadership Position	General Responsibility	What Did I Learn?	How Did I Apply What I Learned?
Quality Manager	Managed QE and laboratory departments in an aseptic drug and device facility (2 plants); interfaced with FDA	Be able to detect problems before they occur, SPC works People run the QMS, not machines Documentation is critical to process understanding	Improved first pass yields Decreased process deviations Organization produced future leaders
Quality Engineer	Performed validations and screening studies	Take the time to set up a good test plan	Developed quality prediction model for defects, developed inspection processes
Engineer	Provided general manufacturing engineering support	Rules and regulations guide the business Engineering is only as good as production	Installed rework systems Installed vacuum dryers Managed safety program

Leadership Position	General Responsibility	What Did I Learn?	How Did I Apply What I Learned?
Professor	Teach college classes	Stay at the top of the intellectual ladder Teach so others can comprehend and apply the information	Senior Professor Global course shell design National: Top ten instructor
Investor	Purchase rental properties	Do the proper research	Increase in number of rental properties
Author	Write Professional and Fiction Books	Write what you both know about and what you have a passion to learn more about. Use information to help others	Wrote books on Cancer and Quality which have been used to help others learn and apply different ways of approaching difficult situations

The Ten Rules

All journeys begin with a destination in mind; take the time to write out what you want your resume to read like in four years – then go out and make that

resume a reality. A quality leader is able to see a destination; is able to see the path that will get the organization there; is able to develop others so the next journey can be led by others – a quality leader expects difficult decisions will have to be made and prepares for those decisions, a quality leader anticipates change and has a contingency plan that is appropriate – a quality leader is a business leader!

The ten rules are my rules; they may not work for you or your organization. My hope would be that you, as a quality leader, would use the best of my ten rules, delete or modify those that do not fit your role or organization and then even add a few more rules. It does not matter if there are 5 rules or ten rules, but what I do believe matters, however, is the order of the rules and the holistic focus – starting with a humble approach to quality leads to the success of the organization and the career of quality professionals.

A QUALITY LEADER:

1. must never lose sight that quality is part of the organization; quality is not the sole reason for the organization to exist
2. must establish a quality system that the organization can understand and implement
3. must understand the rules that govern how the organization must behave
4. must know the products and services that the organization provides; both their use and misuse
5. must not make decisions on over-simplified information
6. must take proper actions in a timely manner
7. gets other leaders to be an active part of the quality systems of the organization
8. must look for signs of change in the organization before the organization experiences the change; then takes the necessary actions to prevent any unwanted anticipated change from damaging the organization
9. understands the organization's quality intelligence and maturity and the relative impact on the quality systems of the organization
10. establishes quality as a career growth path in the organization

The
4-D
Approach

The 4-D approach (4D) is something I share with every organization in which I have been a part of – professional, volunteer or community. This model, simple in its concept, is powerful in its message – disclose issues early and resolution is manageable and viewed positively; withhold issues and the resolution is difficult to manage and is viewed negatively. I contend that following the 4-D preventive (4Dp) model is a sign of a robust quality system – whereas the presence of the 4-D reactive (4Dr) model is a sign of a poorly functioning quality system.

For the 4D model to work there must be a culture of trust. This does not mean significant deviations from approved processes go unpunished; accountability is a tenet of the 4Dp model – accountability with compassion given the voluntary exposure of quality system issues.

Disclosure  **Discovery**

Quality

4- D Approach: Preventive

This approach will enable the organization in the detection and resolution of issues; in a manner that is timely, effective, collaborative and transparent.

Disclose: When you know of an issue tell your supervisor. Failure to discuss an issue just delays the resolution.

Discuss: After the issue is disclosed we can leverage the talent of the organization to develop multiple approaches relative to the issue.

Decide: Given the benefit of a well-designed discussion process, we are now capable of making the decision that is best for all involved.

Document: The final step is to document the process of issue detection and resolution; so others can learn from the process and so we can demonstrate our deep caring for the well-being of those that use our products and services.

4-D Approach: Reactive

This approach will inhibit the organization from the detection and resolution of issues; which can lead to an inference that the organization is unaware of their own issues, at best, and is secretive, at worst.

Discovery: When someone else finds the issue before us we are forced into a reactive mode; surprises are rarely good.

Dictate: Now, instead of being able to discuss the issue we may have the actions relative to the issued told to us; we lose the chance to control our own destiny.

Document: When someone else finds the issue before us, they will need to document the issue from a technical view (what happened) and a management view (why were there not systems in place to detect the issue).

Damage: The documentation of the undisclosed issue by an outside party can lead to a damaged reputation; reputations are earned and maintained over time, with a passion for what is right.

The 4Dp model makes perfect sense in the written format, getting an organization to adopt the 4Dp model is not so easy. I have found that the 4Dp model is best implemented by expressing the benefits of the 4Dp model to the stakeholders of the organization; and conversely the very negative aspect of not following the 4Dp model (i.e. exhibiting the tenets of the 4Dr model). It is sometimes the negative view of the 4Dr model that often can inspire stakeholders to adopt the 4Dp model; but this is only temporary. The full adoption of the 4Dp model takes a series of issues disclosed, discussed, decided and documented in such a manner that stakeholders of the organization see the output of following the 4Dp model as favorable; and, as important, must see those who volunteered the information as none-the-worse for the disclosure of the information. It may take multiple 4Dp cycles for the 4Dp model to become embedded in the culture of the organization, patience is critical in the implementation of the 4Dp approach.

The 4Dr approach, if it exists, cannot be tolerated. This is an approach that must be exterminated from the organization; one way to do this is to take strong action when an issue gone undisclosed is detected by some act of unplanned intervention or luck. An example of a strong action would be, in the lightest manner, a note in an individual's performance file or, in the harshest manner, termination from the organization. In either case, the action must be visible to the stakeholders of the organization; sadly this type of punitive example will often lead the organization to the adoption of the 4Dp approach.

In my field, an example of the 4Dr approach would be the issuance of a regulatory letter. If an outsider assessor, e.g., during the course of an investigation were to discover significant issues that the organization had not disclosed then the assessor might assume the organization to be less than truthful. As such, the assessor may not seek the input of the organization when determining a resolution to the issue detected; instead deciding to dictate a resolution to the organization. In order to assure the organization obeys the dictated approach, the assessor may decide to document the found issues and the dictated action – which can, and often does, damage the organization through public awareness of the issue and through a realignment of resources in a manner in which the organization has little, or no, input. In essence, the 4Dr approach away the ability of the organization to control its own reaction to an issue, dramatically reducing the influence an organization can have regarding future dealings with the assessor and the assessment organization.

Continuing the example above, the 4Dp approach can lead to a much different result. If an outsider assessor, e.g., during the course of an investigation were to discover significant issues and as part of the assessment was to find out that the information had been previously disclosed (or was positioned in such a way to make the detection of the issue easily found), then the disclosure provides the assessor with an initial impression of the organization's honesty and norms. From this point, if the assessor can determine if significant and appropriate discussions were held with the appropriate levels of management and mixture of organizational talent the assessor, most likely, will accept the decisions made as the best possible option available. Then, if the assessor can determine if the discussions led to an implemented decision there would be very little reason to spend time on an issue that would, most likely, not appear on the assessor's assessment report; especially since the organization had documented the issue prior to the assessment, documented the investigation, documented the decision implementation – all in an manner that was visible to others.

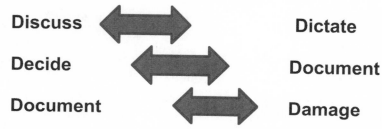

Discuss ↔ **Dictate**

Decide ↔ **Document**

Document ↔ **Damage**

Tributes to Past Gurus

This book would not be complete without a reference to those who have been champions of quality. I have my personal mentors; you may have others – any list will leave out someone deserving and for that I apologize for any significant omissions. That being said, there is one common trait among the great thought leader in the field of quality; which can be summed up by the graphic. You

guessed it – all the great thought leaders in the field of quality are, sadly, dead! Taylor, Shewhart, Deming, Juran, Shingo, Crosby –

dead! Even worse, we still study the approaches of these gentlemen as if their approaches were developed yesterday – Deming developed his 14 points in the mid-1950s – revolutionary for the time – but are they worth such deep review 60 years hence? Are these 14 points applicable to a 21st century organization where information exchange is instantaneous, where global economies and interactions have an immediate impact on the product and

Quality

services provided by organizations? The day has come to move past the thought leaders of the 19th and 20th centuries and develop our own great 21st century quality thought leaders – perhaps a reader of this book will take up this challenge and be the next (and living) thought leader in the field of quality. Yet, as I mentioned, there is value in the historical review of the thought leaders in the field of quality and I do not want to imply otherwise. I have tremendous respect for the quality thought leaders of the past and have learned from and applied their approaches to quality in my personal and professional life.

Any discussion of past quality thought leaders starts with Frederick Taylor; the originator of the field of scientific management. Taylor brought to the field of quality a discipline needed to assure product and service quality was consistent, his workers knew their jobs and were well trained, the work was documented clearly and the job requirements were achievable and fair. In my humble view, all of the quality thought leaders since the early 20th century stand on the shoulders of Taylor; without his structured approach to quality all other quality systems fall apart.

Next in line is Walter Shewhart. Shewhart was the intelligence behind the development and application of control charts, the plan-do-check-act cycle and so much more. It was Shewhart that found ways to communicate complex topics in a manner others could understand; it was Shewhart who found the deep meaning of data that was embedded in natural and special cause variation of a process. Shewhart's text entitled Economic Control of Quality of Manufactured Product should be a required read for anyone interested in quality as a profession.

W. Edwards Deming took Shewhart's work, for the most part, and found a way to communicate the messages in such a way that application was possible. Certainly, Dr. Deming was helped in this quest by post World War II Japan marital law requirements that CEOs and other executives attend his lectures; however Dr. Deming, to his credit, worked to assure those he counseled were able to apply the techniques he espoused. Though some may think Dr. Deming's approaches were at times very liberal minded and not always applicable (e.g. the preference by Dr. Deming to not conduct performance reviews) there are many applications of his theories. I, for one, have found great value in his work on the theory of knowledge; which requires the workers be trained in the theory and science of their work.

Joseph Juran was a giant in the field of quality – his autobiography entitled Architect of Quality: The Autobiography of Dr. Joseph M. Juran is an inspiring read and takes the reader into the

Quality

development of quality throughout the 20th centuries. In this book, Dr. Juran explains, at a deep level, the influences on his approaches to quality – one of special interest to me was an understanding of the different languages of quality within organizations – e.g. between departments, between levels of employees and between stakeholders.

Shigeo Shingo was the pioneer behind making mistake proofing a critical element of any robust quality system. Mistake proofing has been around since the beginning of time; but the passion to implement mistake proofing technics was brought forth by Shingo. Mistake proofing is a planned event; mistake proofing requires using all the processes of the organization (design, operations, sales, marketing, supply chain, et al) to protect the consumer from defective products or services.

Lastly, Phil Crosby put a spark in the quality community with his approach to zero defects; an often misunderstood concept. Crosby understood the realities of work and that perfection was not possible in perpetuity, but he also understood that in order to lessen the chance of a defect there must be a belief that perfection was possible – strive for perfection and achieve excellence – perhaps this is the way to best describe Crosby's approach towards quality.

Quality

Each of the quality gurus mentioned, and many more, have laid the groundwork for this book and countless others. We all owe these gentlemen a debt of great thanks for their devotion to the field of quality. This is not a book about the past; but it felt wrong to ignore the work of others – I know I have oversimplified the work of these quality giants – yet I hope I have provided the focal point of their work – enough to inspire the reader to research further one, or all, of the gentlemen discussed in this chapter. I believe strongly that we cannot live in the past; yet I get that a study of the past is important when we plan for the future. Taking the time to understand Taylor, Shewhart, Deming, Juran, Shingo and Crosby will be time well spent for the quality professional.

SECTION III

QUALITY

SYSTEMS

Problem Solving

Solving problems is a craft; a skill set that is learned through education; refined through mentorship and mastered through life-long application.

One way to visualize this concept is through the field of statistics. The concept of statistics takes a beating each and every day by the statistically uneducated. Statistical analysis, like any other mathematical function, if performed properly cannot be wrong. Yet, it is those same individuals who violate the most elementary assumptions of statistical models, who define populations poorly, who fail to sample properly, who believe that all distributions are normal (a very common mistake) and other mistakes too many to name – who then criticize the concepts and applications of statistics as misleading, inaccurate and, at worst, deceitful. One of the problems with the perception of statistics, in my humble view, is that (most) anyone with access to a calculator believes they are a statistician. If I had the authority to add a required class to high school and college programs it would be a course in statistics; most everyone in their life are exposed to and use the concepts of statistics and having a base knowledge of statistical concepts would go a long way to assuring statistical concepts are applied correctly and are properly understood. The concepts of problem solving shares some of the same concerns as statistics; too few realize that problem solving is an acquired skill gained over years and years of study and application. Yet, take a survey of individuals and, very likely, most will consider themselves to be a good problem solver.

So, once again I enter the realm of the school board and believe that all high school and college programs should have a required course in problem solving; most  everyone in their life are exposed to and use the concepts of problem solving and having a base knowledge of problem solving concepts would go a long way to assuring problem solving concepts are applied correctly and are properly understood. Just as someone would not consider themselves to an accountant, an engineer or a scientist without formal education; nor are those that consider themselves statisticians or problem solvers such unless they have also dedicated themselves to the science and psychology of these disciplines.

Quality

Problem solving, if done properly, is a window into the future. Too often, the process of problem solving is used in a reactive mode – problem solving is as much about preventing a problem as it is about fixing a problem. Now this does not mean all problems can be resolved to the satisfaction of all involved; an example of this is when a marriage dissolves into a divorce – where one of the parties may not be satisfied with the corrective action (divorce) and may not implement the preventive action (e.g. counseling). The corrective and preventive actions resulting from a problem solving process can certainly lead to an entirely different set of problems (e.g. financial concerns associated with a divorce, family issues, et al) which would then need to be recycled through the problem solving process. Problem solving is about segmentation – solving one part of the problem at a time and, over time, solving the much bigger problem (e.g. how to minimize the divorce rate). When emotion clouds a problem solving process (as in the above example), the problem solving process is weakened – this can also happen when an organization has an unhealthy commitment to a process, supplier, talent, product, service et al. As with the example of divorce, there must be careful attention paid to the psychology of problem solving as well much as to the science of problem solving.

Quality

Using the problem solving process I am proposing in this chapter, an organization should be able to recognize a problem at the early stage of the problem solving process – and using the concepts of type 1 and type 2 statistical errors (type 1 – take action, when no action is needed, type 2 – fail to take action, when action is needed) determine the first course of action; followed by thoughtful determination of the proper long term correction and prevention actions. Well, enough on the benefits of problem solving; let's dig into my problem solving model!

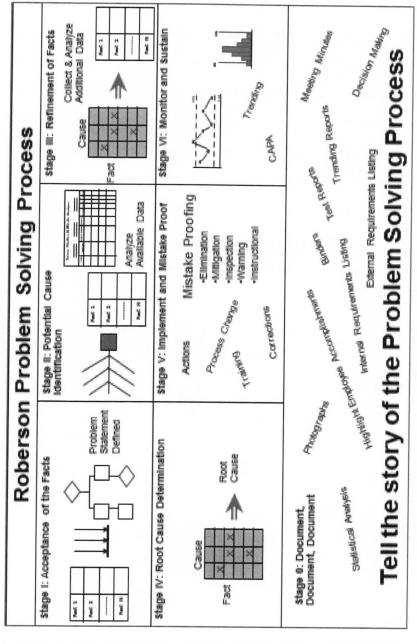

Stage I: Acceptance of the Facts

Before a problem can be solved, the problem first must be recognized and accepted, given this the problem can then be described. For the purposes of this chapter, I am making the assumption that the problem has been recognized and accepted and that the leadership of the organization supports the problem solving effort. The next steps in the problem solving process are the representation of the facts, the development of a time line, followed by flowcharting the process, a review of the representation of facts – all cumulating with the development of a problem statement.

To understand a problem at its deepest level requires there must be a comparison of truthful data. This is not as easy as it might seem; data does not deceive, by itself, but there are ways that data can be misleading – for example data  derived from instruments that are not accurate and precise (to a given standard) would yield misleading (untruthful) information. So the best place to start with defining a problem is with an understanding of the processes in which data will be provided – e.g. accuracy, precision, statistical levels of significance, sampling error,

Quality

et al. This is not an easy task and may seem like this depth is slowing down the problem solving process – but spend any time dealing with non-useful information and data is a certain path to restarting the problem solving process over again and again and again.

After the data integrity concerns have been understood and taken care of, we start the process of looking at facts. It is best to start with a factual representation of the symptoms of the problem and then move on to the more general state of the problem. For example, if problem recognition involves a product defect where there is a hole in the product some (but not all) factual representations might be:

Location and Characteristics

- The hole is located in the in the lower left corner over a range of 1 cm to 2 cm horizontally and over a range of 3 cm to 4 cm vertically.

- The size of the hole in the defective product ranges from a diameter of 0.25 cm to 0.50 cm.

- The hole in the defective product is circular in nature and is smooth around the edge.

Quality

Product Types

- The hole is in 2 product types: product X and product Y.

Operations

- The hole is in products produced on 12/18/2010, first shift at the Williamston manufacturing plant.

- During the time the defect was produced, deviations were noted in calibration and incoming material.

- During the time the defect was produced, differences were noted from standard work regarding cycle time.

- The same product as the defective product is also produced at the Kenosha manufacturing plant.

Customer Experience

- Twelve customers have reported the defect, with the first complaint being on 8/3/2010.

- Each customer reports physical leakage of the product and a break in the sterility barrier.

- Each customer reports no sharp objects came in contact with the product.

The list could go on and on; and it should go on and on! There must be a profound and deep search for the facts; for facts that are obvious and for facts that are not so obvious (which may link to the defect). Even with this much work done, however, the problem is still not ready for definition. The next step in defining the problem is with the development of a timeline; e.g. when the defect was manufactured, when the defect was discovered, what process changes were made before, during and after the defect discovery periods, etc. This is a time of deep reflection and research; there must be a search for events and accurate reflections of when the events became reality. Just because a procedure was issued on a certain date, .e.g., does not mean that it was implemented on the same date. In such a case, it would be appropriate to list both the issue date and the implementation date on the timeline. As with the representation of facts information, the timeline is a living document and may need to be modified during the problem solving process as new information becomes known.

Flowcharting the process in which the defect happened and did not happen is the next step of the problem definition stage of the problem solving process. The flowchart is best done without the aid of existing flowcharts; start with a blank slate using the collective knowledge of the management and the direct line workers. After the flowchart is completed, then the comparison to the existing flowcharts is appropriate – look for differences and note those in the timeline and the factual representations of the defect.

Now, after the facts regarding the defects have been collected, after the timeline and the flowchart have been completed the problem solving team is ready to start asking what it is about the problem that is not known. This list can be, and should be, quite long – keeping the list focused on reasonable unknowns. After the list of unknowns has been completed, there must be a prioritization of data collection activities – which unknowns deserve knowing and which do not. It is best to gather the list of required unknowns, making them known, before the problem is defined. Rushing to define the problem dooms the problem solving process; patience must prevail during this stage even though others may be critical of this time taken to define the problem and will have their own view on the problem definition. Rest assured it is these same individuals who will be even more critical if the problem solving process is not successful. So, what does a good problem definition look like? In the case of our problems (the hole in the left side of the product and the marriage of Mr. and Mrs. Jones), the definition of the problem might look like:

Quality

Product X, used for the purpose of ABC, and produced on date / year, first shift was found to have a smooth radius hole in the upper left corner. This product is also made on other shifts in the same location and in other locations. No defects of this type have been noted during the other time periods or locations. The defect affects the ability of our product to hold its contents, may be unnoticeable to the user at times and, if it were to occur, would jeopardize the sterility of the product contents.

Mr. and Mrs. Jones have reached a point in their relationship where they are not able to communicate and agree on critical life decisions. Although both parties are not in agreement on the best solution to this problem, Mr. Jones will prevail given applicable laws. Mr. and Mrs. Jones, then, seek to find corrective and preventive actions to smooth out the difficulties of a pending and certain divorce.

The problem statement is a guide; it is fine (and often necessary) to modify the problem statement over time given new information.

Stage II: Potential Cause Identification

This stage uses the output of problem solving stage I (one) — Acceptance of Facts –to identify potential causes using factor analysis. Factor analysis, in my view, encompasses the areas of:

1. Human Impact: This factor looks at how humans (stakeholders) affect the representation of facts. An example of this factor would be product misuse conditions, the complexity of a manufacturing processes, the talent of the workforce et al.

2. Design: This factor looks at the elements of design that should have prevented or mitigated the defect.

3. Process and Operations: This factor looks at the elements of process that should have prevented or mitigated the defect.

4. Measurement: This factor looks at the accuracy and precision of the measurement instrumentation used in the collection of information.

5. Management: This factor looks at any biases that might be inflicted into the problem solving process by improper focus or time allocation. Management is different than process; whereas process would include items such as change control, operations et al management looks at the impact management decisions have on the problem solving process.

6. Distribution and Installation: Delivery and Service: These factors look at the state of the product / service once it leaves the control of the organization.

Quality

These factors can then be compared against the established facts, timelines and flowcharts to look for areas where additional information gathering is needed. These are the factors that I like to use on cause and effect diagrams – as opposed to the standard factors of material, methods, manpower and machine (the classic 4M model of manpower, method, materials and machine).

Stage III: Refinement of Facts

In this stage, there is a comparison of stage I and stage II information. It is at this point that we begin to compare the factors identified in the cause and effect diagram to the representations of facts diagram (ROF). Before we can proceed to the contraction diagram in stage IV, we need to determine if the assumptions that were made in stage I and stage II are valid, is there a need to collect additional data, does the data as presented provide an unbiased view of the problem, are we sure we have narrowed down the data and potential causes to the point that corrective and preventive actions will be possible, etc. This takes time and a bit of reflection; again hurry through stage II and you will only find yourself in the next stages with data and information that actually confounds the problem solving process

Stage IV: Root Cause Determination

This stage of the problem solving process is where root cause determination is made; where there is a comparison of causes and ROFs. After the root cause is determined, then the proper corrective actions and preventive actions can be determined.

All of the statements of fact must be supported by the potential cause in order to make the claim that the root cause has been determined. So, if we have 100 statements of fact and a particular cause supports 99 of the100 statements of facts but contradicts 1 of the 100 statements of fact, then we have not found the root cause of the problem. Finding a contradiction allows us to focus the problem solving effort on the most probable causes; e.g. when multiple causes support all of the statements of fact. In this type of situation, we can continue to gather statements of fact to further define the root cause or we could decide to approach the problem given that there are multiple and perhaps confounding root causes relative to the problem. It is at this point that the problem solving team needs to revisit the problem definition − if the problem definition is not sound, if it is more about symptoms than the problem − then the root causes identified will not solve the problem holistically. For example, when a child gets a cold they can be treated with medicine and hot soup − and they will most likely get well, But to solve the problem, keeping the child from going outside without the proper clothing would be the best way to prevent the reoccurrence of the illness.

An example of a contradiction diagram is provided in the diagram below. This example illustrates the level of thought needed to determine root cause and the need for documentation for the contradiction decision.

Statement of Fact	The hole is in products produced on 12/18/2010 first shift at the Williamston manufacturing plant.
Potential Cause	The machine located on the product line where the defect occurred has or had a defective mold.
Factor	Design
Cause = Fact	No
Comments	If the machine has or had a defective mold, the defect would cover 100% of the product and other shifts would have been affected.

Quality

Stage V: Implement and Mistake Proofing

The first step in the this stage is to correct the problem (which includes deploying and measuring the fix), then the implementation of a preventive action – using the concepts of mistake proofing. I have defined the concepts of mistake proofing to be:

Elimination	Mitigation	Inspection
Warning	Instructional	

Providing more detail on each mistake proofing element:

Elimination: This is where the potential for the defect has been designed out of the process or product; it is impossible for the defect to happen.

Mitigation: This is where there are fail safe elements to protect the stakeholders and the product, process or service when the defect does occur. Mitigation may be an inconvenience for the user or other stakeholders of the product or service, mitigation may happen in such a manner that the product becomes unusable – mitigation is a process that is determined by understanding the correct customer and correct stakeholder requirements. An example of mitigation would be the crush zones on an automobile; when the mitigation is deployed the automobile becomes unusable.

Inspection: Inspection can be both proactive and reactive. Proactive inspection happens when there are robust verified and validated processes such that an inspection of the parameters of the operation are sufficient to demonstrate acceptable product or service delivery; also known as parametric release. Reactive inspection is the physical inspection or observation of the defect (as defined by the 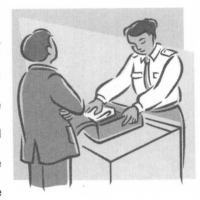 appropriate risk level); in such assuring if the defect were to occur than the organization would detect the defect before the defect reached the correct customer or correct stakeholder.

Warning: This type of mistake proofing concept provides the attentive user a warning of pending problems; e.g. an alarm on a medical device might indicate the device is malfunctioning (whereas mitigation might turn off the device automatically). For a warning to work, the user must be educated on the product or service, must pay attention to the warnings when the warnings occur and must communicate the warnings to the appropriate individuals (though in many cases today, processes self-report [electronically] to the organization that provided the product or service).

Instructional: This type of mistake proofing involves structured

processes to help prevent the defect from happening. For example, an operational procedure would be an example of an instructional mistake proofing tool.

All the elements of mistake proofing must be addressed when the implementation of a root cause action is undertaken. If the mistake proofing element cannot be achieved (e.g. if elimination is not an appropriate option) then the omission of the mistake proofing step should be documented to indicate the reason for such a decision.

Stage VI: Monitor and Sustain

This stage of the problem solving process is where trending and tracking of data is done to assure implementation and mistake proofing activities are effective. Inherent in this stage of the problem solving process are established limits that, when tripped, would initiate the process the review and action. Monitoring is more than just data collection and analysis; monitoring also includes the commitment to sustainment – assuring the corrective and preventive actions continue to be effective over the long term. In order to accomplish the task of monitor and sustain, there must be a well-defined measurement and trending process. This requires understanding the meaning of the data and information at a deep level; e.g. breaking product complaints into specific parts of the product 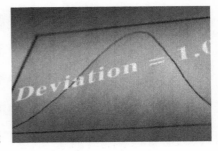 characteristics that have failed as opposed to dealing with the raw number of complaints. The story behind the data must be told in such a manner that others clearly understand the plot; there is not any room for mystery with respect to stage VI of the problem solving process.

Stage 0: Document, Document, Document

This stage is part of every stage of the problem solving process; and as such I have included it first numerically but last in the order of the model. Documentation would include such items as meeting minutes, presentations, accumulation of data and information to support each problem solving stage and more. Organizations should take pride in the problem solving effort; highlighting human achievements. Documenting the problem solving process well leads to organizational learning; while also demonstrating to those outside the organization the in-depth and through process the organization took when addressing the problem. More than likely the problem solving effort will result in a problem solved; but there will be times when the problem returns. Having a well-documented problem solving process helps the problem solving teams redirect and refocus their efforts; and provides those outside the organization with the confidence that the processes of the organization relative to problem solving are robust and sound – and, as such, are deserving of another opportunity relative to determining the problem root cause and the respective corrective and preventive actions.

Closing Thoughts

It is very easy to want to quickly solve and strongly react to a problem – both are signs of an immature problem solving process. Patience, foresight and persistence are the mantras of problem solving – taking the time to understand the problem at its deepest level and then acting in a sequential manner in which actions can be added to, rather than taken back, is critical to assuring the buy-in of others relative to problem solving actions and to assuring the problem solving process is successful.

The tools of problem solving require a methodical and patient approach; require well thought out problem statements and data analysis, require mathematically valid protocols and experimentation and require through mistake proofing applications in order to prevent the reoccurrence of the problem itself. Almost certainly, the problem did not develop over a short period of time so there should not be an expectation that the problem can be completely resolved quickly. As certain, the problem solvers, most likely, did not cause the problem itself – yet there will be plenty of individuals still around the organization who were either directly or indirectly involved in the development and manifestation of the problem. As such, problem solving is a mixture of applying both the

Quality

concepts of problem solving, emotional intelligence and change management (specifically related to organizational culture changes).

I have found, in my career, that having a structured problem solving process is critical to defect understanding and prevention (from the technical view) and in resetting and sustaining organizational culture. Problem solving is a discipline; discipline teaches adherence to established rules and assures consistency of actions and outputs. It is a lot easier to solve the future problems of an organization (and there will be future problems) if the current processes are followed, produce consistent results and the workforce is trained to think in a structured and scientific manner. Now, problem solving processes are not set in stone – there are needs to modify the tools of problem solving to adjust to a particular type of problem. For example, when dealing with a software defect some adjustment to the problem solving model might be needed in order to account for nuisances in how software engineers think about a problem and the complexity of spider code throughout the product. This concept – of a software based problem solving process – provides the fodder for yet another book on quality!

The Importance of Training and Education

One of the greatest mistakes a quality leader can make is the failure to provide for the proper training and education of the organization; a mistake in this area can cause the loss of a competitive advantage for an organization and can easily destroy the legacy of the quality leader. The funds allocated for training and education must be strategically planned and

implanted in such a manner to gain the greatest return for the organization and for the correct stakeholders (i.e. the correct customer, the correct employees, the correct suppliers, et al). The task of defining and implementing the proper training and education opportunities is not easy – there must consideration for:

- the current and future states of the organizations

- the current and future product and service offerings

- the current and future use conditions of the product and service offerings

- the current and future competency of the employees as linked to the current and future organizational state

- current and future product and service offerings

- current and future customer use conditions of the product and service offerings et al.

This decision and implementation process links directly back to the concepts of chapter 1 of this book – the Wisdom to Tradition model.

Training and education must add significant value to the organization and the correct stakeholders. For this to happen the training and education must be both holistic and focused. Holistic training seeks to build the total employee – this type of training is often focused on the softer skills; such as relationship management, negotiation skills, et al. Focused training has as its purpose mastery – e.g. product usage training, software coding training, procedure training [e.g. change control], product user manual training, et al. Education is different than training – training seeks to deliver a message and demand compliance whereas education seeks to provide an understanding of the need for compliance – holistic education and focused education are different from holistic training and focused training. In this chapter we will examine each – holistic training, focused training, holistic education and focused education – examining the proper way to accomplish each with the greatest return.

Quality

Training

Holistic training is about finding a way to change a behavior; providing the organizational view of how a process should operate within the boundaries of the organization. This type of training is often one-sided and rarely utilizes effectiveness checks. This does not mean holistic training is without merit – holistic training has great value given that the holistic training is planned and delivered properly and with sufficient frequency. For example, relationship training is often performed over a short period of time and typically, with one-way communication. The material might be wonderful, but to be effective the employee will most likely have to repeat the training multiple times over an extended period of time – as behavioral changes take time and repetition to become established. This type of training can also be used to reinforce key tenets of the organization – such as the values the organization considers importance. Every correct stakeholder should participate in some type of holistic training annually – it is too easy to forget the proper behaviors or forget the underlying value of the organization without some type of periodic reminder. Holistic training should result in reducing the variation related to understanding of the core tenets of an organization.

Quality

Focused training is about finding a way to secure understanding of a process at such a level that compliance is achieved; in essence focused training is about how to do something. This type of training is often one-sided communication but, different from holistic training, utilizes effectiveness checks. This type of training often does not need to be repeated given that the processes of the organization have remained stable. Focused training (e.g. product usage training, software coding training, procedure training [e.g. change control], product user manual training, et al) utilizes specific examples and constructs to help the correct stakeholder understand the concepts and be able to apply the material. Focused training is about mastering the material to the level that, with experience, retraining is not necessary. Effectiveness checks for focused training might include the tracking of defects associated with a particular process before and after the focused training, the time required for an activity before and after the focused training, etc. Focused training should result in compliance to the policies and procedures of the organization; providing for consistent processes, products and services.

Quality

Education

Holistic education is all about why something happens – to be able to understand the cause and effect relationships relative to a process, a product or a service. Holistic education is typically longer in duration than holistic training and delves much deeper into the topic. For example, holistic training regarding the science of plastic molding might explain the different types of plastic molding operations and discuss the meaning of the process parameters whereas holistic education would explain how the polymer structure of plastics affects the propensity of the plastic to function well in the customer use environment; how changing the parameters of the process might affect the quality of the final product and how to predict problems in the process or product given a set of conditions occurring during a set period of time. A softer side of holistic education would be, e.g., 1) a series of business courses at a university – where the student learns the concepts of the business world in both the theoretical and application environments or 2) information associated with the product use and purpose; e.g. understanding what it is about the product that helps the product attack cancer cells. Holistic education utilizes effectiveness checks to determine the extent of retention of the material covered, the defects prevented over a period of time, etc. – however the time of the effectiveness checks can be quite long as the determination of prevention can be a function of opportunity. Holistic education should develop well-rounded employees who are able to appreciate the systems of the organization and understand the cause and effect relationships of organizational systems.

Focused education is all about how to improve something. For example, where focused training might help an engineer understand how to develop and test software code, focused education helps an engineer understand how to develop better code and better testing scripts. Focused education should result in better process, product and service design – which should result in fewer defects, fewer complaints and a competitive advantage for the organization. As with holistic education, for focused education the time of the effectiveness checks can be quite long as the determination of prevention can be a function of opportunity.

Quality

The Training and Education Cycle

Going a bit deeper into the concepts of training and education, let's link the concepts to a concept I call the strategic training and education cycle.

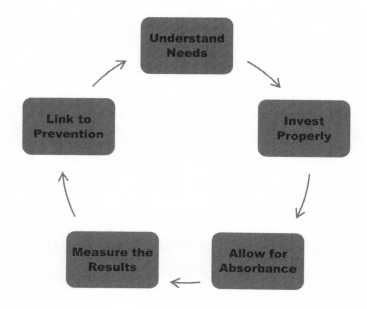

It all starts with a needs analysis; one based on current and future talent competency models. It is critical to separate the desires of the organization and the employees from the needs of the organization and employees. This is not as easy as it might seem, as emotion can often play into this section of the training and education cycle. An example of a training and education need would be one linked to the current product or service or a future version of a product or service. For example, in the field of software, a need might be an understanding of a new software language.

Investing properly is about selecting the correct training and education programs – it is one thing to know what to do; it is quite another to find someone or a process that can deliver on the need. This step involves understanding the structure of the training and education (e.g. in-class or on-line, partial or full days, work outs, testing strategy, et al) along with defining the who and the how of the delivery. Do not underestimate the power of the presenter and the presentation – a passionate well prepared instructor is worth much more than a well-educated and experienced yet ill-prepared instructor.

It takes considerable time and opportunity for training and education to become part of the culture of the organization; there must be allowance for the absorbance of the information. The time allotted for absorbance will depend on the complexity of the material and the opportunities available for application; organizations should, when they train and educate, plan opportunities for application as part of the training and education process.

All processes must be measured; which implies that there is an inherent definition of success or failure. Measurement, with respect to training and education, should not be clouded by how individuals felt about the training or education experience (though this is certainly important) but rather should be primarily focused on the desired outcomes of the training and education efforts. For example, if training is conducted relative to software engineering, the measures should be primarily focused on reductions in software errors, the speed of innovation et al.

All roads in quality lead to prevention – training and education are no different. The results of measurement should lead an organization to an understanding of the ways in which problems could have been prevented in the past or could be prevented in the future. The knowledge gained from the training and education experience, coupled with the information gained absorbance timeframe and the analysis of the metrics are critical inputs into the type of knowledge and information needed to advance the products and services of the organization; a natural link back to understanding the needs of the organization.

Quality

Experienced Based Training

Experienced based training is when an organization artificially sets up conditions to help the organization learn how to work within the established conditions. In my field, an example of this be mock inspections – this is where the organization simulates an inspection by a regulatory agency. This includes hiring someone to act as the assessor (and feeding them with the most difficult questions that can be foreseen regarding the quality systems of the organization), assembling documentation teams, assembling and testing those who will represent the organization et al. This practice helps keep the organization focused on the potential for an inspection; and assures the start-up of any regulatory inspection will go smoothly. This type of activity takes considerable time and resources; but the return is worth the investment when an assessment happens and, even if an assessment does not happen, this type of activity helps the organization stay focused on how the work and documentation of the organization can come under review at any time.

Quality

Train By Example

As a quality leader, I have found it necessary to not only provide for the lifelong organization training and education of the organization but also to practice this process myself. I routinely take professional license examinations to increase my level of knowledge, but also to demonstrate to others in the organization the importance of staying informed, at the highest levels, of the developments in one's chosen field. When leaders learn and apply knowledge, those in the organization see very clearly that the path towards advancement must include a passion of learning. I would strongly encourage any current or future quality leader to dedicate themselves to the concept of learning; and to demonstrate this by taking the time to earn respected and meaningful licenses, certifications, credentials and degrees.

What have you done to inspire others to learn?

Empowerment

I went back and forth on whether to include a chapter on empowerment in this book. This is an extremely complex topics; books have been devoted to this topic alone. I find this topic quite challenging – empowerment is vastly misunderstood by the organization and the workforce; confusing time in a role as opposed to the more important variables of performance, knowledge, education and experience.

Empowerment is not a gift – is should never be such –empowerment must earned through hard work, a deep understanding of the organizational capabilities and strategy and a passion for the customer's long-term well-being. This means that employees will have varying empowerment levels; some employees who have been at the organization longer will have less empowerment than employees who have been at the organization a shorter period of time. This unequal distribution of empowerment can be a source for dissension in the organization and stress between employees. In addition, empowerment that is not managed properly can lead to a lack of change awareness in the organization – one of the most serious problems an organization can have.

One example of empowerment, for me, comes when I am visiting the correct customers. It is important that I recall that commitments I make to the correct customers have an impact on the organization – having an understanding of both the correct customer and organizational needs and capabilities is critical to making sure an organization can keep any commitments that I might make. Now, empowering myself does not mean I make commitments without guidance. I like to think of empowerment as the authority to speak on behalf of the organization, which has been granted to me by the organization under a structured set of conditions – those conditions being defined informally or formally (such as policies and procedures). As my responsibilities have increased over time I would say that I feel less and less empowered to act as an individual. In my early professional days there were numerous areas I could use empowerment; but they were clearly defined and to be honest would not have made a lot of differences if I had made the wrong decision. Today, I would be very unlikely to empower myself without the advice of others as my decisions have a much larger impact on the organization and the correct customer.

As important is an understanding that empowerment does not mean unlimited authority, nor do limits invalidate the concept of empowerment. When I read or learn about organizations that shout as loud as they can "our employees can shut down the line or, our employees are free to always delight the customers". I often wonder if the organization really understands the concept of empowerment –- and worse, if the organization has established in the correct customer's view a level of empowerment that does not exist in the organization. Organizations have limits, so empowerment has limits. I, for one, do not believe the ability to shut down a production line will help make a better product; to make a better product fix the design process. I have come to learn over the years that empowerment is really more about using your responsibility and authority to work within the rules of the organization – make the necessary calls – but more than likely taking the time to consult with others before any empowerment decisions are made. This is not an easy concept to grasp – empowerment involves risk and with risk comes the responsibility of the organization to empower only those who are empowerment ready.

Employees often desire empowerment well before they are ready for empowerment (which is to be expected for the entry level employees and is a disappointment when this happens with the more experienced and savvy employees); a prudent organization works very hard to help employees understand the right timing for empowerment and prepare the employee for the empowerment opportunity. Children are an example of this concept; children often want empowerment (e.g. staying out late, driving the car, et al) well before they have the proper levels of performance, knowledge, education and experience to use empowerment properly – parent know the time is not right for empowerment but the child does not see the refusal of empowerment in the terms of performance, knowledge, education and experience; instead the child take the refusal of empowerment as a personal failure and a failure of the parents (the organizational management) to understand the environment in which the child (the employee) lives and operates. In order to avoid this confusion, there must be a clear set of requirements from which the parents will make the empowerment decision; if this exists then the parent and the child can fairly determine if and when the child has meet the requirements which would allow some level of empowerment. The same holds true for organizations – there needs to be a clear set of rules that govern how empowerment is earned and retained within an organization.

Quality

These rules must address the core elements of empowerment:

1. Performance

2. Education

3. Knowledge

4. Experience

Quality

Performance

The empowerment element of performance requires that employees earn empowerment over a period of time as they (the employee) demonstrate solid and predictable performance; in essence they must be masters of their own job. This requires a clear understanding of job duties and in-depth observations of the employee's performance as related to their job duties. Through the observation process, the organization must determine how the employee will act in situations where there is not a clear action to be taken; where there must be an interpretation of the job duties relative to the desire of the correct customer as linked to the rules, policies and procedures of the organization (which would also encompass any regulations or laws under which the organization must operate). These are telling times for an employee desiring empowerment; decisions are not clear cut and often have to made in the moment – employees that perform well in these situations are the type where empowerment opportunities may be warranted in the future – but this alone is not enough – all four empowerment elements must be satisfied before an employee is able to use the tool of empowerment.

Quality

Education

The education element of empowerment is about how the organization desires to use the tools of empowerment. Organizations that desire to use empowerment must develop an education process that helps employees increase their skill levels relative to empowerment. This type of process would include a clear set of selection criteria for the type of employee that would be good candidates for empowerment opportunities, a mentoring program with employees who have already earned the ability to use the empowerment tools, and training classes on the a) organizational strategy, b) decision making and c) the psychology of the empowerment moment. Empowerment is a journey that starts with strong performance that is then rewarded with an investment in the employee with training focused on what empowerment means; to the correct customer, to the organization and to the employee.

Quality

Knowledge

The knowledge element of empowerment is about knowing the organization – what the organization stands for and the impact of empowerment decisions on the organization – from tactical to strategic, from the impact on the reputation of the organization to how an empowerment action might affect the next correct customer interaction. An empowered employee should not only know the core elements of the organization's strategy but also why the organization selected the strategic approach. This means having a deep understanding of how empowerment actions will affect the organization as a whole (e.g. equal and fair treatment for the correct customers – will the organization be able to repeat the empowerment action for a similar correct customer) to the level of interdepartmental interfaces (i.e. how will the empowerment action affect the activities of another department). Empowerment is about seeking a solution that is the best fit for all; this means the empowered employee must know at a deep level what areas of the organization might be affected by the empowerment decision. This level of understanding comes with a desire by the employee to understand the organization at a the level past that of general awareness.

Quality

Experience

The experience element of empowerment is about the holistic (total) application of the elements of performance, education and knowledge – in an environment where opportunities are provided to the employee in order to provide an experience that the employee can draw upon in the future. This is not easy; this must be a planned event. The organization needs to actively 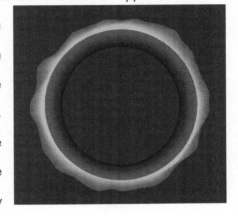 look for experience opportunities for the employee – in order to accomplish this the organization must be able to predict, with reasonable accuracy, when the next empowerment opportunity will happen. Some ways to accomplish this are to understand how the correct customers interact with the organization – some correct customers may present more of an empowerment opportunity than others. Another way to accomplish this is place the employee in an area where empowerment opportunities are likely to occur; e.g. dealing with correct customers that wish to return a product or who wish to report a complaint. With the element of experience also comes the maturity to know when to report the empowerment actions and their impact, using the appropriate channels within the organization. Without this type of reporting, the organization can lose control of its change management process – believing processes to be working one way when in actuality they (the process) are working differently than expected. The element of experience requires patience; employees who do not understand this are not the type of employees who should be empowered by the organization.

Quality

Phased Empowerment

Employees can have empowerment bestowed upon them at one level and be working towards empowerment at another level at the same time; empowerment advancement is a parallel circuit – not a series circuit. Employees who have achieved a level of empowerment within the organization are the type of employees organizations want to  retain – empowered employees are top performers, but more important empowered employees typically have a passion for the well-being of the organization and put the correct customer first. Empowered employees, if developed and nurtured properly, rarely put their needs above the organization or the customer. Empowerment must be earned; if entitlement ever becomes the tag line for empowerment the organization is doomed to inconsistent empowerment decisions (and a loss of change control within the organization) that, eventually, will inconvenience (at best) the correct customer base or will have similar correct customers being treated differently (at worst).

Tenets for a Successful Inspection

It is the inherent nature of quality that assessments are conducted and that assessments have to be managed. During my career in quality I have participated in assessments too numerous to count; during this time I have developed what I believe to be some tenets for successfully treading the assessment waters. In this chapter, I will not expand on the tenets other than to list them and provide a brief explanation – the beauty of the tenets are in their simplicity and, as such, I do not plan to ruin the tenets with needless elaboration. I start the tenets with the following statement:

> "If we are to be successful in our upcoming assessment here are some items that we must do well. This also pertains to our ability to provide exceptional customer service and to maintain our competitive advantage."

Ten Tenets for a Successful Inspection

1. **Tenet 1:** First impressions count; we must show we are prepared for an inspection both technically (in the data we present) and in our actions (the way we present the data).

2. **Tenet 2:** Follow our own procedures; there is no room for error with this requirement.

3. **Tenet 3:** We must know our own surprises and have already reacted properly and instituted preventive action

4. **Tenet 4:** We must never surprise the assessor; so we must have reported issues of concern to the assessment organization prior to the assessment .

5. **Tenet 5:** We must speak the language of the assessor. The harder we make it for the assessor to understand our way of doing things, the more difficult the assessment will become.

6. **Tenet 6:** Our records must be easy to understand. Quite simply, simple processes are the best processes.

7. **Tenet 7:** Our management must be committed to the quality systems; this means having routine reviews of data with subsequent actions.

8. **Tenet 8:** We must demonstrate that we are a learning organization; it is ok to make mistakes as long as we can demonstrate that we have learned from our mistakes. Our mistakes must not repeat themselves. Our non-conforming processes (such as CAPA – corrective and preventive action) are key to demonstrating that we are a learning organization.

9. **Tenet 9:** We must have a variety of process experts; the assessor looks for processes that are understood by the total workforce.

10. **Tenet 10:** We must show appreciation for the assessor and the assessment process. The assessor is there to help us become better at what we do; which helps our customers and the patients we serve make the proper health based decisions.

Quality

This is a short chapter; but hopefully powerful in its simplicity. The tenets of a successful inspection speak to the need for respect towards the assessment process, talking the language of the assessor, following established processes and taking proper actions when mistakes have been made.

Quality

SECTION IV

APPLICATION

Inspection Application

The following pages detail a presentation I made to a Medical Drug and Device Conference in 2010. The presentation demonstrates one way to apply some of the concepts listed in this book. As such, the pages that follow will look a lot like PowerPoint slides.

Strategies for Warning Letter Response and Remediation: Abstract

When medical product manufacturers receive formal letters of warning, it is imperative that the manufacturer respond with a sense of urgency and that credibility with the regulatory authority be reestablished as soon as possible. Establishing an organized documentation trail that demonstrates a comprehensive and timely response and objective evidence of corrective and preventive actions that address root causes is crucial to avoiding further regulatory actions. In addition to addressing each observation, it is often necessary to consider the issue to be systemic, and take a holistic approach when creating an action plan and performing remediation. Correcting fundamental observations without performing a thorough root cause analysis and documenting objective evidence of the corrections can lead to lengthy delays in satisfying authorities that corrective actions have been implemented and found to be effective.

Quality

The Firm Must Accept:

- That a Warning Letter is only indicative of a disease symptom; it is up to the firm to diagnose and treat the disease; to insure the disease does not reoccur.

- That change must occur in the firm's operation processes, communication approach and culture; in a short period of time, using a well thought out strategy.

- That documentation of the activities associated with the Warning Letter must be through, detailed, tangible and well presented.

- It is the responsibility of the firm, as a good corporate citizen, to continue to improve their business; to have a positive effect on their customers and global community WITHOUT ever having to be the receiving end of a FDA Warning Letter.

Quality

FDA Responsibility

- The FDA is responsible for protecting the public health by assuring the safety, efficacy, and security of human and veterinary drugs, biological products, medical devices, our nation's food supply, cosmetics, and products that emit radiation.

- The FDA is also responsible for advancing the public health by helping to speed innovations that make medicines and foods more effective, safer, and more affordable; and helping the public get the accurate, science-based information they need to use medicines and foods to improve their health.

What Is A Warning Letter?

- When FDA finds that a manufacturer has significantly violated FDA regulations, FDA notifies the manufacturer. This notification is often in the form of a Warning Letter.

- The Warning Letter identifies the violation, such as poor manufacturing practices, problems with claims for what a product can do, or incorrect directions for use. The letter also makes clear that the company must correct the problem and provides directions and a timeframe for the company to inform FDA of its plans for correction. FDA then checks to ensure that the company's corrections are adequate.

Quality

Why isn't a [product] taken off the market when a manufacturer gets a Warning Letter?

- Warning Letters generally cause manufacturers to quickly and cooperatively correct problems . . . Warning Letters often help to solve product problems without having to remove necessary products from the market. When necessary, for [product] manufacturers who receive Warning Letters, FDA may withhold approval of a new [product] from that manufacturer until identified manufacturing problems that may affect the new [product] are corrected. In addition, 1) for foreign [product] manufacturers who receive Warning Letters, FDA may refuse to allow the manufacturer's [product] to be imported for sale in the United States until the problems that may affect the [product] are corrected *and, 2) FDA may delay CFG for firms, which may inhibit the export of [product] to others countries.*

- In cases when FDA finds that a manufacturer refuses to fix problems after receiving a Warning Letter, the agency can take additional measures to protect public health. For instance, FDA can quickly issue a press release or consumer alert to notify the public not to use the product. Additionally, FDA can take legal action to seize [product] or to stop a company from further manufacturing and distributing the [product].

4- D Approach: Preventive	4-D Approach: Reactive
This approach will enable the organization in the detection and resolution of issues; in a manner that is timely, effective, collaborative and transparent.	This approach will inhibit the organization from the detection and resolution of issues; which can lead to an inference that the organization is unaware of their own issues, at best, and is secretive, at worst.
Disclose: When you know of an issue tell your supervisor. Failure to discuss an issue just delays the resolution.	Discovery: When someone else finds the issue before us we are forced into a reactive mode; surprises are rarely good.
Discuss: After the issue is disclosed we can leverage the talent of the organization to develop multiple approaches relative to the issue.	Dictate: Now, instead of being able to discuss the issue we may have the actions relative to the issued told to us; we lose the chance to control our own destiny.
Decide: Given the benefit of a well-designed discussion process, we are now capable of making the decision that is best for all involved.	Document: When someone else finds the issue before us, they will need to document the issue from a technical view (what happened) and a management view (why were there not systems in place to detect the issue).
Document: The final step is to document the process of issue detection and resolution; so others can learn from the process and so we can demonstrate our deep caring for the well-being of those that use our products and services.	Damage: The documentation of the undisclosed issue by an outside party can lead to a damaged reputation; reputations are earned and maintained over time, with a passion for what is right.

Quality

Deep Down Look

- Consider each observation systematic, look for deeper cause
- Spend significant time to understand the underlying problems
- Understand why the CAPA process was ineffective
- Use the Warning Letter process to improve; re-learn to track and trend; learn to be preventative

Management Accountability

- Simplify processes; get rid of unnecessary fluff
- Resolve old issues
- Allocate significant funds to the effort
- Reward those who make significant contributions to resolutions to the Warning Letter
- Teach the importance of documentation

Change Management

- Adopt the 4D and Inspection model
- Improve your processes using CAPA; if necessary reinvent your process
- Have practice audits in order to understand areas for improvement
- Have practice audits in order to prepare for the re-inspection
- Remember it's about improving the processes for yourself, not just for the inspection

Quality

Seek Outside Help

- Bring in strong Quality professionals to help

- Make sure outside help installs knowledge and does not take knowledge from organization

Holistic Communications

- Communicate broadly within the organization the status of the Warning Letter remediation effort

- Communicate broadly within the organization the importance of the Warning Letter remediation effort

- Keep FDA updated

- Keep Senior Management updated

- Document, with absolute transparency, in a manner that is easily understood

Personal and Organizational Sacrifice

- Causes personal stress; do not underestimate the effect of a Warning Letter remediation on individuals or the individual's work quality

- Loss of CFG approval can shut down the business

- Long nights and weekend

Quality

Steps Towards A Successful Inspection

1. **First impressions count**; we must show we are prepared for an inspection both technically (in the data we present) and in our actions (the way we present the data).

2. **Follow our own procedures**; there is no room for error with this requirement.

3. We must **know our own surprises** and have **already reacted properly** and **instituted preventive action**.

4. We must **never surprise the inspector**; so we must have reported issues prior to the inspection.

5. We must **speak the language of the inspector**. The harder we make it for the inspector to understand our way of doing things, the more difficult the inspection will become.

6. Our **records must be easy to understand**. Quite simply, simple processes are the best processes.

7. Our **management must be committed to the quality systems**; this means having routine reviews of data with subsequent actions.

8. We must **demonstrate that we are a learning organization**; it is ok to make mistakes as long as we can demonstrate that we have learned from our mistakes. **Our mistakes must not repeat themselves**. Our non-conforming processes (such **as CAPA**) are **key to demonstrating that we are a learning organization**.

9. We **must have a variety of process experts**; the inspector looks for processes that are understood by the total workforce.

10. We must **show appreciation for the inspector** and the inspection process. The **inspector is there to help us become better at what we do**; which helps our customers and the patients we serve make the proper health based decisions.

Quality

The Firm Must Accept:

- That a Warning Letter is only indicative of a disease symptom; it is up to the firm to diagnose and treat the disease; to insure the disease does not reoccur.

- That change must occur in the firm's operation processes, communication approach and culture; in a short period of time, using a well thought out strategy.

- That documentation of the activities associated with the Warning Letter must be through, detailed, tangible and well presented.

- It is the responsibility of the firm, as a good corporate citizen, to continue to improve their business; to have a positive effect on their customers and global community WITHOUT ever having to be the receiving end of a FDA Warning Letter.

Using the Tools of Quality to Battle Cancer

The following pages detail a presentation I made to the American Society of Quality World Quality Conference in 2010. The presentation demonstrates one way to apply some of the concepts listed in this book. As such, the pages that follow will look a lot like PowerPoint slides.

Using Quality Principles To Battle Cancer

Abstract:

Cancer is personal to me. I have had cancer twice – in 1991 and in 2006/2007. During my treatments I used many quality concepts to maintain my mental and physical health. I was fortunate to use medical devices and drugs of which I had either been part of the design or manufacturing team. I will expand on how I used the quality concepts on my journey with cancer; along with how my work in the medical industry became personal to me as I used drugs and devices to save my own life.

Quality

The structure of process:

- helps reduce uncertainty and unnecessary stress; this is important for organizations and for cancer patients!
- helps with the understanding of the difficulty of the journey ahead
- lessens the potential for the oversight of critical information
- helps individuals plan their own journey with cancer

My Timeline

All Is Fine

- 1959: Born Biloxi, Mississippi
- Father in USAF: family lived in MS, MA, NC, FL, AK (3), NE, VA (2), CA, AL, OH, VA
- 1981: Graduated college, started working
- 1989: August 3rd first child was born

The First Cancer

- 1990: December 11th felt a lump on the right side of my neck
- 1990: December 18th, second child was born
- 1991: February 1st, chemotherapy regime (8), followed by radiation (~30)
- 1991: October, end treatment

The Second Cancer

- 2006: September 29th, felt a lump on the left side of my neck
- 2006: October, started continuous chemotherapy (~40 days in the hospital)
- 2007: January, stem cell harvest
- 2007: January, end treatment

Non-Hodgkin's Lymphoma

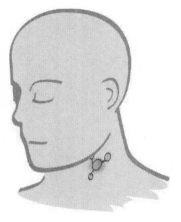

- Lymphoma is a type of cancer that affects white blood cells. One type of lymphoma is Non-Hodgkin's Lymphoma (NHL).

- In someone with NHL, the white blood cells do not behave normally. Instead, they grow and multiply uncontrollably.

- Lymphomas can also form in the bone marrow because that's where white blood cells are produced.

-

Peripheral Neuropathy

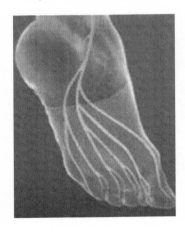

- Peripheral neuropathy is caused by nerve damage.

- Peripheral neuropathy can result from exposure to toxins – such as chemotherapy

- Peripheral neuropathy causes numbness and pain in your hands and feet.

Quality

Process Management and the Link to Cancer

- Processes help maintain focus; they are a reminder of the importance of simplicity

- Processes provide security for the patient, doctors, nurses and caregivers

- Processes help individuals ask better questions and understand those answers at a deeper level

- Processes help avoid missing critical information

- Processes help maintain a focus on the most critical areas

Five Stages of Grief

- Denial and Isolation

- Anger

- Bargaining

- Depression

- Acceptance

- The process which we are about to discuss helped me, and I believe can help others, avoid spending unnecessary time in the first four stages of grief and progressing to the fifth stage of grief.

- Getting to acceptance quickly allows the cancer patient necessary actions that must be taken.

- This process also reduces unnecessary stress and increases their chances of living.

Strategy and Cancer

- Wisdom: Every individual has wisdom based upon the knowledge and experience in a particular area

- Strategy: Top level strategy; developed using the collective wisdom of the organization

- Action: Tactical plans developed to support the top level strategy

- Accountability: Achievement of the treatment plan, on schedule, in a detailed and defensible manner.

- Tradition: Improvements made as a result of the organization's determination are sustained; driving a competitive advantage for the business

- Wisdom: Understand the cancer and yourself

- Strategy: Establish plan to battle the cancer

- Action: Implement the plan; stay the course

- Accountability: Never, never, never quit the treatments

- Tradition: Use the journey of cancer to increase your wisdom; improve other areas of your life and the life of others

Quality

4- D Approach: Preventive	4-D Approach: Reactive
This approach will enable the organization in the detection and resolution of issues; in a manner that is timely, effective, collaborative and transparent.	This approach will inhibit the organization from the detection and resolution of issues; which can lead to an inference that the organization is unaware of their own issues, at best, and is secretive, at worst.
Disclose: When you know of an issue tell your supervisor. Failure to discuss an issue just delays the resolution.	**D**iscovery: When someone else finds the issue before us we are forced into a reactive mode; surprises are rarely good.
Discuss: After the issue is disclosed we can leverage the talent of the organization to develop multiple approaches relative to the issue.	**D**ictate: Now, instead of being able to discuss the issue we may have the actions relative to the issued told to us; we lose the chance to control our own destiny.
Decide: Given the benefit of a well-designed discussion process, we are now capable of making the decision that is best for all involved.	**D**ocument: When someone else finds the issue before us, they will need to document the issue from a technical view (what happened) and a management view (why were there not systems in place to detect the issue).
Document: The final step is to document the process of issue detection and resolution; so others can learn from the process and so we can demonstrate our deep caring for the well-being of those that use our products and services.	**D**amage: The documentation of the undisclosed issue by an outside party can lead to a damaged reputation; reputations are earned and maintained over time, with a passion for what is right.

Quality

Knowledge of Cancer: 4-D Approach

In my 1991 and 2006/2007 cancer, I was able to use the preventive approach as I discovered my own cancer.

- (Disclose) informed my medical team of the issue
- (Discuss) had detailed and well-reasoned discussions relative to my treatment options
- (Decide) chose a treatment plan that worked and fit my goals
- (Document) 1991: entered Marquette MBA program; in 2006 and 2009 I continued teaching; both allowed me to show others the humanity of cancer

Knowledge of Cancer: 4-D Approach

In most cases the reactive approach is utilized with someone gets cancer:

- (Discovery) medical team informs individual of the cancer; individual is surprised and shocked
- (Dictate) due to urgency doctor dictates treatment
- (Document) due to urgency individual cannot share their journey with others
- (Damage) potential long term psychological damage as a patient feels left out of the cancer decision process

Quality

Quality Leadership and Cancer ... A quality leader:

1. must never lose sight that quality is part of the organization; quality Is not the sole reason for the organization to exist.

2. must establish a quality system that the organization can understand and implement.

3. must understand the rules that govern how the organization must behave.

4. must know the products and services that the organization provides; both their use and misuse.

5. must not make decisions on over-simplified information.

6. must take proper actions in a timely manner.

7. gets other leaders to be an active part of the quality systems of the organization.

8. must a) look for signs of change in the organization before the organization; then make the necessary change.

9. establishes quality as a career growth path in the organization.

10. understands the organization's quality intelligence and maturity and the relative impact on the quality systems of the organization.

Quality

A person with cancer:

1. must never lose sight that they are part of a global community, they are not any more important than anyone else in the global community.

2. must establish a treatment plan that they can understand and can be implemented.

3. must understand the rules that govern cancer and cancer treatment.

4. must know the capabilities and limitations of the medicines of cancer.

5. must take the time to understand the complexity of the cancer and the cancer treatments.

6. must take proper actions in a timely manner; such as notification to the medical team of physical and emotional abnormalities.

7. must use the cancer to teach others the importance of life.

8. must look for signs in their body and mind continuously; changes can affect the immune system.

9. must use the cancer to grow as an individual.

10. must understand that not all individuals, family members, and friends will be able to accept the reality of the cancer.

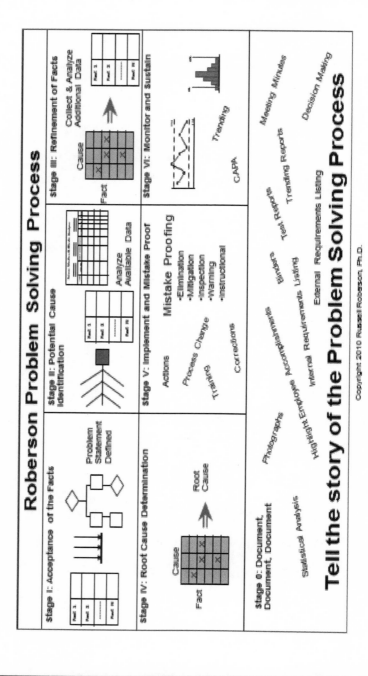

Quality

Stage I: Acceptance of the Facts

– Representation of the facts (ROF); taking a wide and deep look

– Development of a time line

– Flowcharting the process

– Review of the representation of facts

– Develop problem statement

Stage II: Potential Cause Identification

– Identify potential causes using factor analysis:

- Human Impact

- Design

- Process

- Measurement

- Management

- Installation, Delivery and Service

– Analyze Available Data

Stage III: Refinement of Facts

– Comparison of stage I and II information

– Collect and analyze additional data

– Modify ROF, timeline and flowchart as necessary

– Revisit potential causes

Stage IV: Root Cause Determination

– Comparison of causes and ROFs

– Determine root cause

– Treat root cause as a symptom; then determine proper corrective actions and preventive actions

Stage V: Implement and Mistake Proofing

– Corrective Action

  • Deploy and measure fix(es)

– Prevention Acting: Utilize the concepts of mistake proofing

  • Elimination

  • Mitigation

  • Inspection

  • Warning

  • Instructional

Quality

Stage VI: Monitor and Sustain

— Trend and Track appropriate data to assure implementation and mistake proofing activities are effective

Stage 0: Document, Document, Document

— Document the steps of the problem solving process

— Keep meeting minutes, presentations, et al that are generated as part of the problem solving process

— Use good paper; take pride in the problem solving effort

— Highlight human achievements

Note: Step 0 happens in every stage of the problem solving process

Utilizing the Problem Solving Model to Battle Cancer

Stage 1 - Cancer has Invaded My Body

- **Representation of Facts**

  - Affects me physically

  - Affects my family et al emotionally

  - Has no known cause

  - Is aggressive NHL

  - Flowcharted life activities and concluded it was not my fault

  - **Defining the Problem:**

  - *DEATH*

Stage 2 - What Could Cause Me to Die

- Stopping treatments

- Being timid, failing to take actions ahead of the cancer

- Failing to prepare myself mentally

- Failing to set up a friends and family network

- Acting as if I have become the more important than others

- Giving into the cancer; accepting that it has a place in my body

- Failing to get professional help / counseling

- Failing to build a great medical team

- Failing to trust the medical team I assembled

- Underestimating the physical pain of cancer

- Stopping work, stopping being a father, stopping being a husband

Quality

Stage 3 - Refinement of Facts

- 1991 Stage II NHL

    - Spread to chest; outpatient treatments

    - 2005 Stage I NHL

    - Spread to neck; required hospitalization

Stage 4 - Root Cause Determination

- Key Issues (Root Causes)

    - Not having a full understanding of NHL and treatment affects

    - Not securing counseling

    - Not preparing my family and friends for the cancer

    - Etc.

    - Key Issues led to creation of Creed, Vision and Motivational Story (which was shared with medical team, caregivers, family, et al)

Stage 5 - Implement and Mistake Proof

- Talked to other cancer patients

- Studied NHC

- Changed my mind set on pain

- Planned for the future

- Accepted the cancer but never valued the cancer

Quality

Stage 6 - Monitor and Improve

- Tracked my attitude
- Tracked the pain
- Tracked the good moments; learned from the bad moments
- Let others know of my progress

Quality

Cancer Creed

- ➢ I believe that no action on my part (physical, emotional, intellectual, or spiritual) caused my cancer. I accept no responsibility for the cause of this cancer.

- ➢ I believe that there is not any logical reason for my cancer; I will not waste my time searching for a reason why I have cancer.

- ➢ I believe that I will become a better person by experiencing the journey of cancer; but I also believe that I need not have cancer to constantly improve my worth to myself, family, or society.

- ➢ I believe that I am not any more important, or less important, a person because I have cancer. I am the same person now as I was before cancer; and will be the same person after cancer.

- ➢ I believe that I will beat the cancer that has invaded my body, and I will do so in a dignified manner. This cancer attacks me, my family and my friends. I will not let such an unworthy opponent affect me, my family, or my friends physically, emotionally, intellectually, or spiritually.

- ➢ I believe in the abilities of my medical team to care for my physical body, the support of my family and my friends to care for me emotionally, myself to care for me intellectually, and the power of God to care for me spiritually.

Quality

Cancer Vision

Cancer invades your body without your permission; it is a thief in the night, scared to face you on equal ground.

Cancer invades your heart and your soul, of that there is no doubt. Cancer wants to change you; cancer wants your dignity.

Choose to make cancer a good part of your life; choose to make cancer a moment that your life-light never shown brighter or with more passion.

This is not something cancer wants; it is not something cancer can control. Making cancer a good part of your life robs the thief of his power. Making cancer a good part of your life moves the fight to an equal ground.

Choose to use cancer rather than letting cancer use you.

Choose to live.

Motivational Story – A True Story

Once upon a time, a man ran a race 17 miles in distance along a mountain trail. The man was physically fine, but not in the best shape to run such a race. As the race began, the man was enthusiastic, but after a while he tired. So the man went from running to walking; but the man did not quit. He kept moving forward. Soon he regained his strength and began to run again; but soon he would tire and begin to walk. Along the way the man slipped, but he got up and continued. After a while the man found himself alone, as those who started with him were either far ahead or far behind. The man did not care; he focused on finishing the race he had started. When the man reached the 15 mile point he had exhausted himself physically. Intellectually he knew he had no more to give, that he had gone past the point his body could endure. It was at this point the man realized something about himself; that even though he was past his limits he could endure, he could continue. The man focused on finishing the race, putting all his energy toward that goal. It was not easy as the last two miles were the hardest stretch of the race. The man was no longer running; he was now walking at a very slow pace; but the man was constantly moving forward. The man never took a step backward and never thought about quitting. The man had gone too far to quit. Four hours after starting the race, the man finished. He was exhausted, but he had finished. He had finished last among those that had finished (many had dropped out along the way), but he had finished. The man felt good about himself, not for his physical accomplishment, but for his mental accomplishment. The man had been past his point of endurance but had continued, and he had finished the race.

That man was me. And as I finished that race, I will finish this race with cancer. At times things may seem bleak, and without hope, but rest assured I will finish the race; and by finishing the race I will have won the race.

Quality

Family Helps

Life

After

Cancer

- Focus on the preventive part of the 4-D model

- Other events in life are not so scary

- Every day must be **EARNED**; your life must honor those that did not survive their own cancer journey

It takes more than desire to beat cancer - to beat cancer you need a strategy - a strategy that brings dignity and honor to the cancer patient and to their caregivers. This book humbly, suggests a strategy to do just that

.
Cancer is a kick in the gut, an unforeseen knock-out punch. Russell Roberson, a two-time non-Hodgkin's cancer survivor, helps others battle cancer through a q unique approach that produces both dignity and honor for the cancer patient and their caregivers. In this book understanding and accepting cancer, developing a strategy to

live, understanding the realities of cancer, understanding the rewards of cancer, understanding the end game for cancer (not for the patient, instead for the cancer) and life after cancer are discussed.

Provided at the end of the book are worksheets for the cancer patient and caregiver to develop and monitor their own cancer journey - a journey of dignity and honor.

http://www.amazon.com/Cancer-Journey-Russell-Leo-Roberson/dp/1450501370/ref=sr_1_1?ie=UTF8&qid=1303086602&sr=8-1

REVIEW: This clear and concise read enlightened me on the key rolls of the cancer patient, family and friends. The book explains how a cancer patient enables constructive progress by applying appropriate leadership skills in and around friends and family. The book also enlightens family and friends on how to meet their roll and responsibilities. The fundamentals offered are applicable far beyond situations involving Cancer.

Making Your Home Life Better

The following pages detail a manner in which the concepts of this book may be used in a less familiar manner but one a great importance – how to make your home life better. I have used many of the examples to follow during my class lectures; I have found that if I can relate a topic to home life the concept is sometimes easier to grasp and understand – and is often recalled easier than a technical business related examples.

Quality

Wisdom To Tradition Model	Application
Wisdom: Every individual has wisdom based upon the knowledge and experience in a particular area	Understand the maturity of the family, intelligence, team skills, financial savvy, et al.
Strategy: Top level strategy; developed using the collective wisdom of the organization	Establish goals; e.g., establish the plans for a summer adventure (immediate), the purchase of a car (short-term) and for affording college expenses (long-term)
Action: Tactical plans developed to support the top level strategy	Set in place specific actions that each family member can take; from research to financial diligence. Establish metrics to determine if each action item is progressing as intended.
Accountability: Achievement of the treatment plan, on schedule, in a detailed and defensible manner.	Evaluate each family member against the action items set. Taking into account the concept of Wisdom, the strategy and action times should have been set such that the family bought into the strategic concepts are were capable of achieving the plans.
Tradition: Improvements made as a result of the organization's determination are sustained; driving a competitive advantage for the business.	Working together as a team on family focused activities builds the family strength and creates memories that will sustain family members in the future. Additionally, the wisdom can transfer to future generations.

Quality

Situation:

My step-son asked me recently to fill up the gas can that we use for the snow-blower. I thought this was an unusual request given that this was in March and rarely did we have a snow in March that necessitated the use of the snow-blower. Yet, I did not want to discourage my step-son from wanting to help out in the rare instance a snow came in March that would require the use of the snow blower.

Later that evening, I looked out into the back yard and in our fire fit there was a roaring fire – which I estimated to be at least 3 feet to all – and next to the fire was the very gas can that I had filled up earlier in the day. It became very clear to me that my step-son had never wanted the gas for the snow blower; but instead a fuel for a very large fire that he was planning on building.

When I asked my step-son why he had not talked to me about building such a large fire and using gas as the fuel his reply was as expected – that if he had asked I would have said no – which I would have (relative to using gas as the fuel, but not to the fire – though I would have insisted on a smaller fire). As such, we were in the 4-D Reactive model – starting with discovery.

Here is how the situation might have gone using the 4-D preventive approach:

Disclose	I would like to build a large fire tonight.
Discuss	Sure – how large a fire; how do you plan to start the fire; are you going to use the fireplace wood or wood you get from somewhere else; how will you make sure your friends do not get hurt when they are around the fire? One of the responses from my son might have been – well, I plan to get a gallon of gasoline and soak the wood that we use from the fireplace, then build the fire to about 3 feet tall and then keep the gas can next to the fire in case I need more fuel. This would have been a point of discussion.
Decide	Together we could have decided to pick out the dry wood from the fireplace wood pile, could have gone to the store and purchased some fire starters and could have designed a fire that was tall; but maybe not 3 feet tall.
Document	Documentation in this example is not paper based; but more mental – we should be able to recall that we worked this situation out and know that in the future we could do the same again for similar type of situations.

... but here is how it actually turned out ...

Discovery	I looked out the window and saw a roaring fire, with the very gas I had purchased for the snow blower being used as a fuel. I also realized that my step-son had not been up-front with me on the need for the gasoline.
Dictate	I walked outside and removed the gas can from the vicinity of the fire; told my step-son to reduce the height of the fire and instructed that group of friends move back a safe distance from the fire (not a popular move by any means).
Document	I realized that I could not be as trusting for items that do not make clear sense to me in the future; for my step-son he realized that it would take time to rebuild some of the trust lost between us due to this incident.
Damage	There was a moment of tension and embarrassment; followed by a discussion on the importance of clear communication.

This is just a simple example of the 4-D model applied to family life; my contention is that if the 4-D model were used consistently that most all problems could be avoided.

4- D Approach: Preventive	4-D Approach: Reactive
This approach will enable the organization in the detection and resolution of issues; in a manner that is timely, effective, collaborative and transparent.	This approach will inhibit the organization from the detection and resolution of issues; which can lead to an inference that the organization is unaware of their own issues, at best, and is secretive, at worst.
Disclose: When you know of an issue tell your supervisor. Failure to discuss an issue just delays the resolution.	Discovery: When someone else finds the issue before us we are forced into a reactive mode; surprises are rarely good.
Discuss: After the issue is disclosed we can leverage the talent of the organization to develop multiple approaches relative to the issue.	Dictate: Now, instead of being able to discuss the issue we may have the actions relative to the issued told to us; we lose the chance to control our own destiny.
Decide: Given the benefit of a well-designed discussion process, we are now capable of making the decision that is best for all involved.	Document: When someone else finds the issue before us, they will need to document the issue from a technical view (what happened) and a management view (why were there not systems in place to detect the issue).
Document: The final step is to document the process of issue detection and resolution; so others can learn from the process and so we can demonstrate our deep caring for the well-being of those that use our products and services.	Damage: The documentation of the undisclosed issue by an outside party can lead to a damaged reputation; reputations are earned and maintained over time, with a passion for what is right.

Quality

Quality Leadership ... A quality leader:

1. must never lose sight that quality is part of the organization; quality Is not the sole reason for the organization to exist.

2. must establish a quality system that the organization can understand and implement.

3. must understand the rules that govern how the organization must behave.

4. must know the products and services that the organization provides; both their use and misuse.

5. must not make decisions on over-simplified information.

6. must take proper actions in a timely manner.

7. gets other leaders to be an active part of the quality systems of the organization.

8. must look for signs of change in the organization before the organization; then make the necessary change.

9. establishes quality as a career growth path in the organization.

10. understands the organization's quality intelligence and maturity and the relative impact on the quality systems of the organization.

Quality

A family leader:

1. must never lose sight that they are part of a family, they are not any more important than anyone else.
2. must establish ways of running the family that the family can understand.
3. must understand the rules that govern how the family must behave – and clearly communicate those rules to others in the family.
4. must know the family members at a deep level and be able to reasonably predict how family members will act in a given situation.
5. must not make decisions on over-simplified information – in the case of a family this means the willingness to listen.
6. must take proper actions in a timely manner – in the case of a family this means making decisions that fit the attention span of the family member.
7. gets other leaders (such as grand-parents, aunts and uncles, et al) to be an active part how the family is run.
8. must look for signs of change in the family; then take the necessary actions to prevent any unwanted anticipated change – in the case of a family this might mean keeping close track on the activities of children, who the children are friends with, having access to social media used by children et al.
9. establishes the family as a safe-haven and a way to model future generations.
10. understands the family's intelligence and maturity – in order to assure the strategies of the family link well to the capability of the family to achieve the strategy.

Quality

Now let's look at an application of the SWEATT model.

Strengths

Focus	Measure	CV	MP
Finances	Amount of funds secured in an emergency savings	$10K	$9K
Vacations	Number of family vacations taken per year that allow total relaxation	2	0
Activities	The amount of significant activities each child is engaged in (e.g. band, sports, scouting, etc.)	1	0

Weakness

Focus	Measure	CV	MP
Arguments	The number of arguments (in a week) over agreed upon chores (e.g. yard care, laundry, et al).	3	1
Cleanliness	The number of times (in a week) a parent becomes so upset with the cleanliness of the home that severe action is required (e.g. this room will be cleaned up "right now")	5	1
Grades	The number of children in the home that make a grade of C in any academic subject during a school year	3	0

Quality

Excellence

Focus	Measure	CV	MP
Sponsor a Large Family Gathering	The amount of large family gatherings per year (e.g. a summer picnic inviting aunts, uncles, nieces, nephews, siblings and parents)	0	1
Coordinated family activities that are small in nature	The amount of times during the year the family (together) engages in common events (such as movie nights, going out to dinners, going bowling et al)	6	12
Pay off debt	The amount of unpaid debt (absent of the house) – removing debt will allow a more relaxed atmosphere in the family and will allow achievement of other goals of the family	$35K	$5K

Threats

Focus	Measure	CV	MP
Divorce	Are the parents considering or pursing a divorce	No	Yes
Drugs	Are any of the children involved with the use of drugs	No	Yes
Finances	The amount of time in a year that the monthly credit card bill exceeds $4000	2	3

Quality

Actions

Focus	Measure	CV	MP
Purchase a car	Amount of cars needed for the family to function well	5	6
Establish a savings strategy	Amount in savings to accommodate current and future significant expenses (e.g. college, vacations, graduation gifts, et al).	$65K	$85K
Lay the ground work for a large family gathering two years out	Amount of monthly communication with family members vetting the idea of a large family gathering.	0	4

Team

Focus	Measure	CV	CV - 1
Leaders	Length of Marriage	20	19
Children with jobs	Number of children with paying summer jobs	3	1
Children at College	Number of children attending college full time	3	3

This is a simple example of the SWEATT model applied to family life; hopefully this example is useful in demonstrating the application of the SWEATT model.

Quality

SECTION V

CLOSING

A Final Thought or Two

A Final Thought or Two

Summarizing a book of this type brings to mind the vast amount of material and information that has not been covered – e.g. leadership styles, customer satisfaction models, statistical applications, supplier quality, the importance of a robust quality management system, the need for advanced educational opportunities in the field of quality, and more. Perhaps these topics can be chapters in another book on the concepts of quality; they are not forgotten – just not included in this book.

My hope is that you have will have found this book helpful in the development of your own quality strategy – perhaps a thought or two from this book will be the seed that helps you develop and refine your own approach towards quality. I am not so naïve to think that the ways I

have proposed are the only ways to view quality – but the ways espoused in this book have been my model and, from what I have heard from others, a basis for the quality models of other.

If there is an overlying theme of this book it is that the way we define quality has to change – quality has to boldly step into the 21st century; we have to develop quality leaders who view quality as a life-long profession – who are passionate about the field.

Quality is way too complex to be defined by a random customer or a random stakeholder. Organizations have to seize control of how quality is defined and help the correct customers and correct stakeholders understand that by their releasing control of how quality is defined that the quality of the products and services they receive will actually get better. Those of us in the quality profession have to look for ways to make the models of quality more business focused – the SWEATT model with movement points demonstrates a way to take a qualitative tool and make it quantitative – with a strong link to the overall quality strategy of the organization. There is no doubt that with the innovations of the 21st century (speed of information exchange, advanced technology, et al) that those of us in the field of quality must rethink our view of world – we owe it to the society in which we live to put forth our best thoughts and approaches towards quality – who knows you may one day have to depend on your own dedication and passion

towards quality to help save you own life – just as I have had to do –
twice!

What a journey – we are nowhere close to the finish line –
which is what makes this journey relative to the quality principles so
much fun!   Let me close this book with one final thought:

Customers, by their mere existence, have not been
bestowed with the divine right to define quality.
Organizations, by their deep knowledge of the products and
services they provide, are in the best position to define
quality.   For organizations to be successful they must
become solely responsible for defining quality; in the process
educating the correct customers and the correct
stakeholders of the organization in such a way to assure
acceptance of the organization's definition of quality over
any other definition of quality.

Dr. Russell Roberson

DIAGRAMS

OF THE

BOOK

Quality

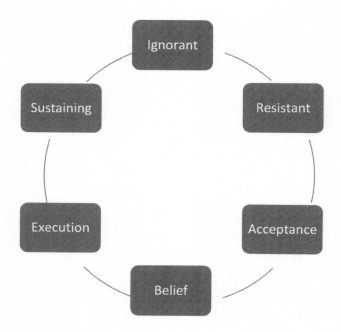

Quality

SWEATT Table

MP	
CV	
Measure	
Focus	

Notes:

Quality

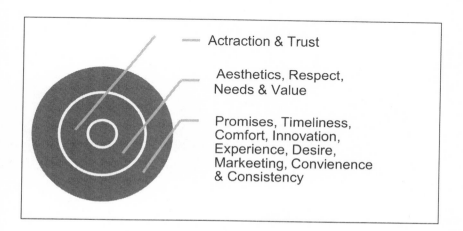

Actraction & Trust

Aesthetics, Respect,
Needs & Value

Promises, Timeliness,
Comfort, Innovation,
Experience, Desire,
Markeeting, Convienence
& Consistency

Quality

A QUALITY LEADER:

1. must never lose sight that quality is part of the organization; quality is not the sole reason for the organization to exist
2. must establish a quality system that the organization can understand and implement
3. must understand the rules that govern how the organization must behave
4. must know the products and services that the organization provides; both their use and misuse
5. must not make decisions on over-simplified information
6. must take proper actions in a timely manner
7. gets other leaders to be an active part of the quality systems of the organization
8. must look for signs of change in the organization before the organization experiences the change; then takes the necessary actions to prevent any unwanted anticipated change from damaging the organization
9. understands the organization's quality intelligence and maturity and the relative impact on the quality systems of the organization
10. establishes quality as a career growth path in the organization

Quality

4- D Approach: Preventive

This approach will enable the organization in the detection and resolution of issues; in a manner that is timely, effective, collaborative and transparent.

Disclose: When you know of an issue tell your supervisor. Failure to discuss an issue just delays the resolution.

Discuss: After the issue is disclosed we can leverage the talent of the organization to develop multiple approaches relative to the issue.

Decide: Given the benefit of a well-designed discussion process, we are now capable of making the decision that is best for all involved.

Document: The final step is to document the process of issue detection and resolution; so others can learn from the process and so we can demonstrate our deep caring for the well-being of those that use our products and services.

4-D Approach: Reactive

This approach will inhibit the organization from the detection and resolution of issues; which can lead to an inference that the organization is unaware of their own issues, at best, and is secretive, at worst.

Discovery: When someone else finds the issue before us we are forced into a reactive mode; surprises are rarely good.

Dictate: Now, instead of being able to discuss the issue we may have the actions relative to the issued told to us; we lose the chance to control our own destiny.

Document: When someone else finds the issue before us, they will need to document the issue from a technical view (what happened) and a management view (why were there not systems in place to detect the issue).

Damage: The documentation of the undisclosed issue by an outside party can lead to a damaged reputation; reputations are earned and maintained over time, with a passion for what is right.

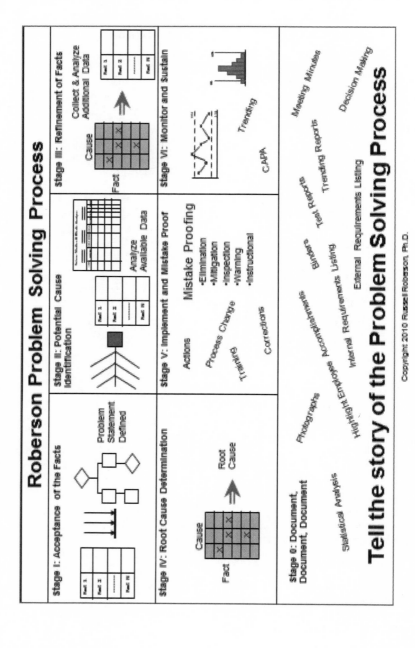

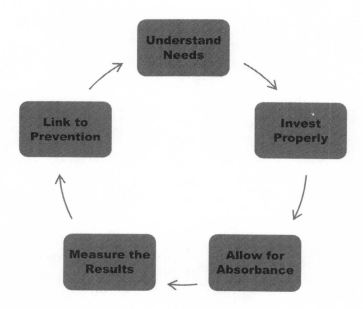

Quality

Steps Towards A Successful Inspection

1. **First impressions count**; we must show we are prepared for an inspection both technically (in the data we present) and in our actions (the way we present the data).
2. **Follow our own procedures**; there is no room for error with this requirement.
3. We must **know our own surprises** and have **already reacted properly** and **instituted preventive action**.
4. We must **never surprise the inspector**; so we must have reported issues prior to the inspection.
5. We must **speak the language of the inspector**. The harder we make it for the inspector to understand our way of doing things, the more difficult the inspection will become.
6. Our **records must be easy to understand**. Quite simply, simple processes are the best processes.
7. Our **management must be committed to the quality systems**; this means having routine reviews of data with subsequent actions.
8. We must **demonstrate that we are a learning organization**; it is ok to make mistakes as long as we can demonstrate that we have learned from our mistakes. **Our mistakes must not repeat themselves**. Our non-conforming processes (such **as CAPA**) are **key to demonstrating that we are a learning organization**.
9. We **must have a variety of process experts**; the inspector looks for processes that are understood by the total workforce.
10. We must **show appreciation for the inspector** and the inspection process. The **inspector is there to help us become better at what we do**; which helps our customers and the patients we serve make the proper health based decisions.

Quality

About the Author

Dr. Russell Roberson is the Vice-President, Quality and Regulatory Affairs, for a medical company. In this global role, he works to assure products and services are designed, manufactured, distributed and  serviced properly. This includes responsibility for an extensive portfolio of healthcare software products in both the medical device (e.g. pharmacy, imaging, electronic medical records and prescription management products) and non-medical device areas (e.g. financial and data privacy products) that are affected by different global regulations and standards. Dr. Roberson is a frequent speaker at global conferences (sponsored by both professional associations and governments) presenting on topics such as software design processes, regulatory affairs, and quality management systems. Since 1996, has been an adjunct college professor; teaching course in the area of quality, strategy, ethics and mathematics. Dr. Roberson also serves on the national board for his college fraternity.

Quality

Dr. Roberson has been recognized with the highest performance award his organization can bestow and has been recognized as the outstanding Biosystems Engineering alumni from his university. Dr. Roberson is a licensed professional engineer, holds professional certifications in the areas of engineering, auditing and management, is active in several professional societies and is on the national board of trustees for his college fraternity. Dr. Roberson has publications in many areas and is the author of two books; in the areas of leadership and cancer management. Academically, Dr. Roberson holds a doctorate degree in Business Administration and Management, a MBA degree, a Master of Science degree in Mechanical Engineering and a Bachelor of Science degree in Agriculture engineering.

Dr. Roberson lives in Kenosha, Wisconsin with his wife, Linda. Together they have five children – Alex, Blythe, Nathan, Brandon and Jordan; along with a Beagle named Crichton.

If you would like to learn more about Dr. Roberson, visit www.russellroberson.com.

Quality

Quality

Made in the USA
Middletown, DE
24 March 2018